D0787079

Modern African Writers

General Editor: Gerald Moore

Peter Abrahams

Peter Abrahams

Michael Wade

Evans Brothers Limited

Published by Evans Brothers Limited
Montague House, Russell Square
London WC1B 5BX

Evans Brothers (Nigeria Publishers) Limited
PMB 5164, Jericho Road
Ibadan

First published 1972

Photoset and printed in Malta by St Paul's Press Ltd

CSD 237 28772 2
PB 237 28779 X   PRA 3063

Modern African Writers

Now that some of the initial excitement and misunderstanding sur-rounding African literature in English and French has begun to subside, it has become clear that it includes a small but growing number of writers who may be called 'serious'. I apply this word not simply to the tone of their books, but to the quality of their commitment to literature, to their sense of themselves as artists with a special and difficult role to fulfil, rather than just as people who happen to have published a book or two.

So much of the critical reception of this literature has been piece-meal, scattered and occasional that it isn't easy for the reader to determine who these writers are, what they have written, or what is the sequence and pattern of development of their work. In the present series, one volume will be devoted to each selected writer and will discuss his work critically, chronologically and con-sistently. In this way, the reader will be able to look at the writer's work as a developing whole or, if he prefers, turn to the chapter dealing with a particular book and see what the critic has to offer there. For one aim of this series is to reveal something about the present state of criticism in this field, as well as something about the work of its major writers.

No single school or method of criticism will be favoured in the selection of contributors to the series. Critics of this literature, both African and non-African, have themselves been subjected to in-fluences as various as existentialism, negritude, structuralism and detailed textual analysis in the Anglo-American tradition; the series will doubtless reflect this variety of method and approach. Like-wise, the selection of authors to be studied will strive to reveal strength and interest wherever they exist, without enlisting itself for or against any particular movement. In this way, the series should enable itself to respond to every major development in African literature and criticism.

G. M.

Contents

The Author

Michael Wade grew up in South Africa. He came to England in 1964, and studied at the universities of London and Sussex. Since 1967 he has been lecturing in the departments of English and African Studies at the Hebrew University of Jerusalem. In the field of African literature he has published articles on Amos Tutuola, Peter Abrahams and William Plomer.

Acknowledgments

The publishers are grateful to the following for permission to reproduce the extracts in this book:

John Farquharson Ltd for extracts from Peter Abrahams' works: *A Night of Their Own*, published by Faber and Faber; *A Wreath for Udomo*, published by Faber and Faber; *Dark Testament*, published by George Allen & Unwin Ltd; *Mine Boy*, published by Dorothy Crisp & Co.; *Return to Goli*, published by Faber and Faber; *Song of the City*, published by Dorothy Crisp & Co.; *Tell Freedom*, published by Faber and Faber; *The Path of Thunder*, published by Faber and Faber; *This Island Now*, published by Faber and Faber; *Wild Conquest*, published by Penguin Books Ltd.

Curtis Brown for the extracts from *Down Second Avenue* by E. Mphahlele, published by Faber and Faber.

Praeger Publishers Inc. for the extracts from *The African Image* by E. Mphahlele, published by Faber and Faber.

The publishers regret that they have been unable to contact the copyright holder of the following passage, but will be very pleased to rectify the omission if any information is forthcoming:

Mhudi by S. T. Plaatje, published by The Lovedale Press.

The photograph of Peter Abrahams on the cover was supplied by Radio Jamaica and that of the author by Joanna Spence.

Introduction

Peter Abrahams is a Coloured South African. Coloured takes
a capital 'C' because it stands for a distinct, statutorily defined
group of people in the weird racial set-up that encloses South
African society. Abrahams defines the term on the second page
of his autobiographical *Tell Freedom*: 'Coloured is the South
African word for the half-caste community that was a by-
product of the early contact between black and white.'[1] It is
legally separate from the white, Asian and African groups
and numbers about a million and a half people. Like all non-
whites in South Africa, Coloureds have no genuine civil or
political rights, though their closeness, at the light end of the
spectrum, to the white group is a politically sensitive matter
and is frequently traumatic on the individual level.

Abrahams was born in Vrededorp, Johannesburg's largest
Coloured and Asian slum, on 19 March, 1919. The Coloured
community in the Transvaal is smaller than the parent group
in the Cape and generally confined to the urban areas. It is self-
contained, fairly endogamous, and hypersensitive to racial
issues, though the emergence of a fair-sized bourgeoisie (since
Abrahams' time in South Africa), combined with the draconian
legal consequences of protest, has made for political quietism.
The Coloureds, in terms of day-to-day life in the Transvaal,
probably have most contact with Indians and least with
Africans. The first language of Coloureds at the Cape is usually
Afrikaans, in a mild dialect form: in the Transvaal, or specifically
in Johannesburg, it is more likely to be English.

Abrahams describes his ancestry in the following terms in
Tell Freedom:

> My father came from Ethiopia. He was the son of land-
> owners and slave-owners. He had seen much of Europe before

[1] *Tell Freedom* (Faber and Faber, London, 1954), p. 9.

he came to South Africa. In after years, when my mother talked about him, she told wonderful stories of his adventures in strange parts of the world ... My mother was the widow of a Cape Malay (a product of the East Indies' strain of the Coloured community) who had died the previous year and left her with two children.[1]

When Abrahams was still a small boy, his father died, and he was sent to live with distant family connections in the trying conditions of the 'native location' of a rural village called Elsburg. After some time he returned to Johannesburg where he played, fought, worked, and then went to school for the first time at the age of eleven. But three years later the great depression forced him to seek work once more, and by a stroke of luck he found employment at the Bantu Men's Social Centre, a haven for the small educated African middle class, as office-boy in the Pathfinders, the black section of the Boy Scout Movement. While there he enrolled in a correspondence course, and later became a boarder at the Diocesan Training College, Grace Dieu, near Pietersburg in the Northern Transvaal. The first step towards joining the non-white elite had been taken.

While with the Pathfinders, Abrahams had discovered the works of American negro authors in the library of the Bantu Men's Social Centre; he began to write poetry, inspired by Keats and Shakespeare, as well as du Bois, Countee Cullen, Langston Hughes, Sterling Brown, Claude McKay and other negro authors of the period. His first poems were published in *The Bantu World*, a white-owned newspaper catering for non-white readers, while he was at Grace Dieu.

The next step was South Africa's best school for non-whites, St Peter's Secondary School, Rosettenville. Ezekiel Mphahlele gives an interesting glimpse of Abrahams during his time there in *Down Second Avenue*:

I remember him vividly talking about Marcus Garvey, taking it for granted we must know about him. And dreamily he said what a wonderful thing it would be if all the negroes in the

[1] *Ibid.*, p. 11.

world came back to Africa. Abrahams wrote verse in his exercise books and gave them to us to read. I admired them because here was a boy writing something like the collection of English poetry we were learning as a set book in school. I remember now how morose the verse was: straining to justify and glorify the dark complexion with the I'm-black-and-proud-of-it theme.

There was a Jewish couple who lived near the school. The man was stocky and had ginger hair, the woman was full blown in a family way. Somehow Peter made friends with them, and they often came to the school to see him. He gloried in this friendship in a way that puzzled us and filled us with awe. 'He has white friends, you know,' the boys said whenever they talked about Peter. I regarded him as a conqueror. I had a vague feeling that his opinion of Marcus Garvey typified him as someone who was always yearning for far-away places. He used to tell us that he wanted to show the white man that he was equal to him. That frightened me a little and I did not think about it those days.[1]

At St Peter's Abrahams made his first social contact with whites, and was initiated into left-wing politics, in which he was active in Johannesburg, Cape Town and Durban until his departure from South Africa as a member of the crew of a freighter about the time of the outbreak of the second world war.

After two years at sea Abrahams reached England, where he worked first for a communist book distributing agency, and then as a member of the editorial staff of the *Daily Worker*. He published his first full-length book, a collection of short stories entitled *Dark Testament*, in 1942, breaking with the communists at about the same time. He became a member of the small circle of African students and intellectuals that included Kwame Nkrumah and Jomo Kenyatta, and helped to organize the 1946 Pan-Africanist Conference in Manchester. He subsequently lived in France for a couple of years, and then returned to England. His reputation as novelist, journalist, and a sort of spokesman on the race issue was steadily growing.

[1] E. Mphahlele, *Down Second Avenue* (Faber and Faber, London, 1959), pp. 128–9.

In 1952 the London *Observer* sent him back to Africa to report on the colour question in Southern Africa and Kenya. The series of articles he produced attracted wide attention, and was published simultaneously in France.

In 1957 the Colonial Office commissioned him to write a sort of popular history and human topography of Jamaica, which was published in 1957 as *Jamaica: An Island Mosaic*. In 1959 Abrahams and his family went to live there, and they have been there ever since. He works for the Jamaican Broadcasting Commission, and is also a staff writer for *Holiday Magazine*.

Peter Abrahams is a novelist of ideas. He writes about the machinery of politics and power, but he uses his considerable grasp of this area of activity to serve his central interest, which is the problem of individual freedom in contemporary human affairs. All his novels except one—the most recent—are set in Africa, and all but one of these in South Africa. He was the first non-white South African since S. T. Plaatje to publish a novel in English, and the first to write fiction in an idiom that was essentially West European. As a result of this he exerted an enormous inspirational influence on the first generation of Anglophone writers in other parts of the continent; Cyprian Ekwensi, James Ngugi and Okot p'Bitek are among those who have testified to this as a matter of their personal experience, though it seems likely that at least in the latter cases it was the fact of his books being published—and by an English publisher—rather than their content, that constituted the real spur. It is possible, and I would say likely, that without the influence of the American Negro writers of the 'twenties and 'thirties as mediated through Abrahams' work, as well as the influence of that work itself, the initial development of literature in English in Nigeria and Kenya would have taken rather a different course.

It should be stated at the outset that Abrahams' ability as a writer of fiction is in the middle range, and the grandiose claims made for his work from time to time by propagandists of African literary culture have been misguided. He is a skilful, if

4

flawed, writer, and there is evidence that he finds the writing of fiction arduous. What is most apparent about his fiction is the complete sincerity and honesty of the author. He has not chosen an easy path; he feels every word he writes and seems incapable of writing conscious pot-boilers. The subjects he returns to again and again in his fiction are the problems which have most exercised—and come near to paralysing in the process—the liberal mind in the West since the end of the second world war. They are the problems of how to reconcile the liberal conscience to the unpleasant consequences of necessary action; how to resist inroads made into the integrity of the individual, especially where these inroads are the results of justified attempts to set others free, to put them on the road to the liberal goal of individual fulfilment. Abrahams invokes and even to some extent typifies the liberal dilemma of the twentieth century.

The story of his ideological development is fascinating if only because it is in a way so common; it is the story of Western literature from the 'thirties to the present day. Like Auden, Spender, Day Lewis, Abrahams began as a Marxist, a 'committed writer', directly involved in political activity; and like them he developed away from communism in the direction of bourgeois liberalism, and now seems to hold the sanctity of the individual and the preservation of his freedom as the only political values worth regarding. Unlike Auden, Spender and Day Lewis, he is a child of the slums, who experienced intense deprivation during youth and adolescence, he owes his success to a mixture of sheer ability, hard work and luck. His moral and intellectual commitment to the values of liberal humanism, and his percipient awareness of the extent of the crisis confronting these values, come from his personal experience of situations in which they have failed, in which they were powerless to protect the natural aspirations of the dark child of a plural society.

Abrahams' development as a novelist falls temptingly but naturally into three broad phases. In his earliest work he is overtly influenced by a Marxist political perspective, and not surprisingly, though rather uncomfortably, his writing falls into the broad category of social realism. This is evident in *Dark Testament*, and his first two novels, *Song of the City*, and *Mine Boy*, both of which deal with the theme of urbanization and the polarity between traditional rural existence and modern industrial town life.

The Path of Thunder, a novel about miscegenation (obligatory for South African writers) constitutes an uneasy transition. The trouble is, basically, that Abrahams' instinctive commitment to individualist and liberal values insists in breaking through the Marxist intellectual framework. In any event, during this period Abrahams' political allegiances were primarily to the causes of African freedom and independence.

The 'nationalist' phase, related, perhaps, to a need to subject his commitment to Africa to a careful historic scrutiny, embraces the historical novel *Wild Conquest* and the novel of contemporary African politics, *A Wreath for Udomo*. This latter is, like *The Path of Thunder*, something of a transitional case; in it, Abrahams has begun to deal with the themes which interest him almost exclusively in his last phase to date: the problem of action and the exercise of political power in relation to the moral values of liberal humanism and the natural desire of the individual for freedom and fulfilment.

Race is apparently an important concern of his last two novels, *A Night of Their Own* and *This Island Now*: but in fact the real focus of concern is the plight of the West twenty-odd years after the end of the war, especially in regard to the difficulties facing the individual, beleaguered by the forces of big business and the corporate state. Abrahams sees the crisis of individual freedom as the most urgent issue facing mankind, and he explores it through a variety of its aspects: but essentially his two most recent novels constitute a process of self-examination, an inspection of the ideological and moral choices he has made and the position he has adopted, in relation to the contemporary reality. Not surprisingly, his characteristic honesty leaves neither the writer nor his chosen values of liberal humanism in a particularly comfortable state: at the end of this latest phase in his development, his vision is pessimistic.

6

It is the progress of this development and the nature of this commitment that we shall be examining in this critical study of Abrahams' fiction. It is a paradox characteristic of our times that Abrahams, hailed as an Anglophone apostle of negritude,[1] the propagandist of Pan-Africanism, and most widely known simply as an 'African novelist' or a 'negro writer' (which last he most emphatically is not) should possess so universal a commitment to the cause of mankind.

---

[1] See Janheinz Jahn, *Muntu, an Outline of Neo-African Culture*, translated by Marjorie Grene (Faber and Faber, London, 1961), pp. 211, 228–9; and Janheinz Jahn, *A History of Neo-African Literature*, translated by Oliver Coburn and Ursula Lehrburger (Faber and Faber, London, 1968), p. 92.

I

Dark Testament and *Song of the City*

Peter Abrahams' first published book was a collection of reminiscences and short stories called *Dark Testament.* It appeared in 1942. In the short autobiographical note entitled 'I remember . . .' with which the book opens, Abrahams claims that the stories and sketches were written between 1930 and 1938, which would mean that the earliest were produced when he was eleven years old and had, by his own account, only just begun attending school.

The stories are naïve and gauche, containing little of literary merit. They are the outpourings of a talented but untrained and unwordly adolescent. There does not appear to be a concrete distinction between the reminiscences, which occupy half the book, and the stories. They are all set in South Africa, preoccupied with the subjects of race and colour, and beset by the same faults, the most obvious being an uncontrolled subjectivity of tone, which is saved from becoming egocentric by the genuine innocence and lack of false sophistication which characterize the stories themselves.

If there is a linking theme, as distinct from common location and subject matter, it is the experience of failure, loss and disillusion. The environment is deprived and hostile, which is true to the author's youthful experience, and it seems likely that he is not altogether aware of what he has to express. The consistency with which experiences of dissolution, failure, breakdown and loss appear in the stories far outweighs the essentially contrived optimism of the socialist propaganda stories in the second half of the book: the uncontrolled sentimentality does not altogether obscure a one-sidedly bleak and pessimistic vision of life.

In the opening sketch, 'One of the Three', the hero describes the fates of three childhood friends, beginning by dividing them according to their aspirations. Tommy is the most conventional. Worst of all he fears poverty, and he wishes to become a teacher, reward his parents for the sacrifices they have made on his behalf, marry the simple girl who adores him and make a secure and comfortable home with her.

Johnny's ambition is 'to see the world', and the narrator intends to 'wander about the country and learn to know my people, and try to earn my living as a writer'.

After leaving school they go their separate ways, having agreed to 'keep in touch'. Three years later the narrator is summoned by a letter from Tommy to a reunion: Johnny is due to return from his sea travels. The hero finds Tommy's marriage a bitter wreck, his mother dead and his father vanished, and Tommy himself paralysed by dissatisfaction and fear.

But the 'fine sensitive Johnny' has fared even worse.

> Life had beaten Johnny. All the fire and force had gone out of him. His fine brown eyes, that used to sparkle with defiance when things were black, were dull and lifeless. He had come home, he said, to try and see himself as he used to be . . .[1]

Johnny's inevitable suicide destroys the relationship between the narrator and Tommy:

> Things were black with Tommy. He was afraid of insecurity, but the keeping up of appearances was getting him down. And always when we were together Johnny came and weighed heavily upon us. Tommy and I agreed not to see each other again. We both felt it would be better that way. Fighting ourselves was bad enough; if we had to fight Johnny too it might be too much for us.
>
> It is one of the saddest things I remember.[2]

The paragraph around which the whole sketch revolves possesses a significance which persists throughout this collection

---

[1] *Dark Testament* (George Allen & Unwin, London, 1942), p. 15.
[2] *Ibid.*, pp. 15–16.

and, it is possible to argue, well into Abrahams' novelistic career. It evokes precisely the nature of his situation: unfortunately, he is tempted to expand on it more than once in this book.

> My life was pretty much the same. Poverty, want of a woman's companionship, and the other things which the non-European South African of education knows so well. There were the three of us. Tommy, Johnny and myself.[1]

The sketch sets the tone for those that follow, though it is one of the better ones in that the element of sentimentality in it is fairly controlled. Loss, disintegration and ultimate defeat are the themes it introduces, and they persist throughout the remaining stories. In 'Brother Jew', the young refugee from Nazi Germany, Izzy, shows the narrator his unpublished writing, then disappears mysteriously. The death from tuberculosis of Ellen, her grandchild whom she has nursed from babyhood to the point where she is about to become a teacher, is also the death of hope for Aunt Margaret, in a world so distorted that love takes the shape of the hump on her back. (The story is called 'Love'.) In 'The Old Watchman', the young articled clerk's life is blighted when the girl he loves is forced by economic necessity to marry her father's creditor: first she gives herself to him for three days, however, only telling him they must part forever at the end. The pattern of this story is hope—false fulfilment—loss. The articled clerk ends up as a night watchman.

'Henny and Martha' is probably the best socialist solidarity sketch in the book. In it the unhealthy climate of a white slum in Cape Town is evoked to suggest the poison of race which has polluted the political atmosphere. Henny and Martha, working-class intellectuals, together with a 'mixed' group of friends defy both poverty and prejudice through love and socialism. Death claims first Henny, then Martha, and finally the narrator, whose love for Martha has reclaimed him from the

---

[1] *Ibid.*, p. 14.

inevitable drift to crime and personal dissolution. So even this gain is balanced by the loss of life. It is noteworthy that even in this slight and sentimental tale the rigours of socialist realism are tempered by the inclusion of a perfectly recognizable form of Christian love. The style of this sketch and one or two others is sub-Runyon, with the author trying to capture the rhythm and vocabulary of Cape Coloured working-class speech and use it as a narrative medium. It is unsuccessful, as a comparison with almost any of Alex la Guma's short stories will show.

The remaining stories include a study of Boer anti-semitism in a rural village—the hero, an urbanized Afrikaner, is rejected by his family when he saves the son of the Jewish shopkeeper from being beaten to death; a short story in which socialism saves the relationship between a factory girl and her teacher boyfriend who has taken to drink and gambling as a result of losing his job; and two long and lurid stories about sex, loneliness and isolation, written in a mood of all-consuming sentimentality which Abrahams, fortunately, soon abandoned.

Two of the most subjective of the sketches are significant in relation to Abrahams' ideological development. They illustrate that his adherence to Marxist politics even in South Africa was at no stage free from reservations, and the grounds of these reservations are particularly interesting in that they suggest a consistent and continuous line of development operating from the very beginning of his writing career. The sketches are entitled 'Lonesome' and 'Saturday Night'. In 'Lonesome' the narrator describes rather incoherently a train journey from Johannesburg to Cape Town, including an incident the significance of which is obviously intended to be portentous but is, in fact, completely unclear. The 'action' culminates in an encounter with one of the Cape Town comrades, a girl with whom the narrator, out of loneliness, falls a little in love, and to whom he pours out his adolescent frustration and sense of isolation:

> She did not understand. I know she thought I was a little mad. That I was a defeatist. That I had sold out the Movement.

Funny, huh? Well, it's true. The Movement. People living in shacks. People begging for a living.

Young intellectuals feeling utterly impotent.

They don't see. And they say, 'Don't, comrade; that's defeatism.' What do I care about defeatism when I am feeling lonesome? What do I care about anything when I need human companionship and sympathy and am told that all will be well *after the* . . .

What about a bit of *now*?

Nigger with a brain? Nigger thinking? No. I'm sorry to disappoint you. I'm scared to think. I will go mad if I think. Those others who are mad are thinking these things. They have passed them on to me. I told her these things. A little companionship. Not to discuss anything. Not to hear that I am a promising young writer for the Movement. Not to be told that they think my book is going to be good. Not these things. Not to be told that there is going to be a Mass Meeting and that I must give the crowd of my best.

What about a little bit of warmth? Someone to hold in my arms? Someone to love and lie down with when I am tired?

Young intellectual? Young fool would be better.

I told her these things. Sitting in a non-European café where we went so that it would be all right.

I was a little bit in love with her; or rather, with her company. She could understand, and could give me sympathy, and then interest me in the Mass Meeting. But I guess she wanted to get away to go to a show. So we rushed through the tea, and again she told me the Movement was doomed if young intellectual leaders like myself were becoming defeatist. What did the comrades in the other countries do?

They at least had someone to talk to. Some woman to understand. Sex can be got in the street. But companionship is something like a religion. A God.[1]

It is already a question of the individual in an environment beset with traps and pitfalls—new ideologies and groupings which avoided the necessity for coming to grips with the old and dominant one of race through intellectual dishonesty;

[1] *Ibid.*, pp. 59–60.

which consequently avoided seeing human beings as individuals with different needs and desires. The final section of 'Saturday Night' describes a young writer sitting alone and isolated in a slum room in Vrededorp, unlike the vivid stream of humanity pursuing pleasure in the streets below:

He listens to the familiar noises for a while. Drunken brawls and curses. Loud swearing. People running away from the pick-up. Boys whistling to girls. Little children playing in the street.

He buries his head in his hands. He remains like that for some time. Then he lifts his head and shakes it, and turns to the type-writer. There is a sheet half covered with writing in the machine. He types one word, then beats it out. He concentrates hard and leans forward over the machine with his fingers ready. His eyes brighten. Then suddenly he sighs and gets up, holding his head with both hands.

'What's the use of any bloody thing? . . . What's the use of knowing what's wrong with the system? . . . What's the use of being alive if you can't do any bloody thing because of your colour? It's all very well to say I've got to think of the Movement only . . . But, Jesus! I don't ask much! I ask for company. Real company! How can I do any bloody thing when I'm going mad? . . . Mad over this hell of loneliness. They'll grumble if I haven't got the report ready, but Christ, I'm human too! Where are they now? Some in the picture houses, some at dances, some having interesting discussions round a fire, eating all they want, contented, and here I am . . . Comrades! And them saying there's too much of race among us non-European comrades. Revolutionists! God!'[1]

The needs of the individual, once again, come before the ideological demands of the political group. There is little doubt as to which side of this conflict claims the writer's passion; and in the light of it, even less surprise when, later, he opts so conclusively for the individual rather than the ideological conception of man the social being.

---

[1] *Ibid.*, pp. 68–9.

Other characteristics of Abrahams' world with which the reader of his novels becomes thoroughly familiar make their first appearance in these pages. The most notable are the powerful, even dominating, female figure, who reduces the male characters to the level of ingratiatingly feckless schoolboys; and the peculiar combination of sentimentality and violence that emerges at its most distasteful in the middle period of Abrahams' writing, in *The Path of Thunder, Wild Conquest* and *A Wreath for Udomo.*

Few of the stories and sketches in *Dark Testament* transcend the category of juvenilia: but they contain the seeds of virtually all the mature author's commitments and preoccupations. And the theme of loss is surely the most consistent and pervasive one in all of Abrahams' works.

Abrahams' first novel, *Song of the City*, was published in 1944. It is an immature work, clumsy in dialogue and almost completely lacking conviction in characterization; the language is cliché-infected and the structure disorganized. But it also initiates certain themes which develop in complexity throughout Abrahams' later work, and it is informed by a quality of youthful ardency and sincerity which augurs well for the integrity of Abrahams' later achievement. Novelists of ideas need to be sincere, even when conviction has long given way to a helpless awareness of complexity and confusion. *Song of the City* confronts issues head-on with the certainty of innocence, but at the same time one of Abrahams' most clear-cut convictions is that the world is not made up of black and white. This is also a good augury; this conviction, with increased maturity, becomes a genuine awareness (though it is rather theoretical at this stage—one feels, somehow, that he has not yet reached the point of reacting to actual situations in terms of their real complexity).

Two story-lines emerge—barely—from a matrix that is crowded with characters and incidents. One is that of Nduli, known as Dick, who makes the classic odyssey from traditional rural life to the big city; and the other is the disintegration of the marriage of the Minister of Native Affairs to his English wife, seen against the historical background of the violent debate which led up to South Africa's decision to declare war on Germany in September 1939. There is, as we shall see, an arbitrary and coincidental connection between these two lines of plot: but the novel is weighed down by so much unnecessary feather-bedding both in character and action that the force of the rather subtle major point—the absence of any other kind of link between Van der Merwe (the Minister) and Dick (the native)—is almost entirely smothered.

Abrahams' decision to take up the theme of urbanization was both courageous and obvious. Though it had been extensively used by white South African authors, the only honest and sympathetic treatment of any literary merit had been William Plomer's *Ula Masondo*, published in 1927. But Abrahams' purpose exceeded that of Plomer: writing from a different kind of commitment to the South African scene, fresh from recent and intense political activity within the non-racial left-wing movement, he was determined to explicate the human realities of the phenomenon in political terms. And, in this, he was right, since to ignore this level would constitute a falsification, and to treat it with Plomer's subtlety would have been beyond the range of Abrahams' powers and would also have necessitated writing from a point of view—that of the articulate and urbane white liberal—that lay outside his experience. Point of view is everything in Abrahams' novels, and it is a level on which his natural and somewhat transparent honesty seldom, if ever, fails him.

The story of Nduli is simply narrated: he leaves his tribal village, applies for a 'pass' at the nearest town where he is renamed by the policeman, catches the train to Johannesburg (though he has to walk the last twenty miles, because he hasn't enough money for the full fare), finds work as a houseboy in the home of the family of Professor Solomon Ashe, a Jewish philosopher of liberal views, and sleeps in a 'compound', an urban hostel for African workers. The inevitable experiences befall him: he falls in love with the voluptuous Basuto girl who works as maid for the Ashes' neighbours: policemen attack him in the street without reason, brutally demanding to see his 'pass'; he is arrested after a dance and sentenced (after being beaten) for violating the pass laws, to 'one pound or seven days'. Daisy, his girl, pays his fine; while awaiting trial in prison, he meets a young politicized African who had shown no fear of the white policeman, told the other prisoners that the white man's purpose was to make them fear him, and fertilized the seeds of change in Dick's mind. He goes back to his tribal home but soon finds the attraction of the city has become an organic part of him: so he sets out on the return journey.

This may sound hackneyed and obvious, but Abrahams writes with considerable moral earnestness, and translates this quality into a steadfast though unsuccessful attempt to 'get inside' the character and perspectives of Dick himself. This is where his technique differs most from Plomer's (and this is true, again, of a similar and more successful treatment of the theme in his next novel, *Mine Boy*). Plomer's sympathetic rendition of his African heroes rests largely on the ascription of romantic, almost Rousseauan simplicity and innocence to their mental processes. On the basis of these entirely European concepts he creates from his African characters men and women who stand physically and spiritually in superb contrast to his comic, corrupt and vicious whites. Abrahams, on the other hand, while accepting the convenience of a *tabula rasa* approach to Dick's sensibility in relation to urban experience, sets him firmly on the road to integration with the European cultural matrix: there is nothing distinctively 'African' about the thought processes which begin his political education. For Abrahams it is not (as for Plomer) a matter of refreshingly fundamental difference, of a basic rejection of the rules of the game the non-whites are forced to play: rather, it is a matter of opportunity being made available, from which the non-whites' entry into the game will develop naturally on the same terms as the whites. And this is a position which Abrahams holds consistently throughout his novelistic career, except at the very end, where he shows signs of radical disillusion but cannot accept any of the obvious alternatives or suggest original and better ones. The one development that takes place in Abrahams' position is the later emergence of a firm attitude towards—or rather against—'tribalism', traditional society and its influences. In *Song of the City* obviously Dick's rural, traditional origin is meant to stand as a counterweight to the new life and new sensibility. But it is very badly realized. Dick himself is wooden enough as a character; but the 'old man', the 'old historian', the 'old mother' and the 'young women' who constitute his briefly and none too vividly described tribal background are completely inorganic. Abrahams doesn't even try to flesh the bones of his cliché of tribal life and thus loses the opportunity of achieving a dramatic tension between urban and rural, traditional and modern in the soul of his hero. His assertion of the conflict that supposedly rages there is merely a badly-written gesture in the right direction:

> Yes, the old men would be sitting round the fire and talking about the old days. The days before the white man came. And dreaming about the wars they had fought and about the great deeds that had been done in those days. And the young people, there were very few of them left, but some would be listening to the old men. Others would be out hunting for rabbits. Yet others would be lying on their backs and chewing grass and looking up at the moon. They would be dreaming of the big cities and the big things they were going to do.[1]

Dick's most fervent desire after meeting the African trade unionist in prison is to seek confirmation from his tribal elders of the new wisdon of not fearing the white man. He even writes them a letter, asking their opinion. But they prefer, he finds when he goes back at the end of the book, to continue to dwell on the past. For him that is no longer possible:

> Mnandi was dead. He had been home for three days now. The sickness was leaving his body. Walking among the sheep on the hillside and among the cattle grazing in the valley, and being among his own people, away from the white man, all that had helped to take the sickness from his body. Yes, there had been

---

[1] *Song of the City* (Dorothy Crisp & Co. Ltd, London, 1943), p. 71.

great sickness in his body when he had left the city. Enough sickness to kill one man. It was all gone now. And the dream of Mnandi was gone too. It was good to be with his old mother again. To eat the food she made and listen to her voice. And it was good to be among the old men; to hear their tales of battles and glories of the past. And to go into the fields and hear the young maidens singing while they worked. All this was good. It helped to take the sickness out of his body. But why was the sickness still there in his mind? Why could not that go also? When you are with your people sickness leaves you for your people are always good to you; well, the sickness of the body had done: why not the sickness of the mind?[1]

Mnandi is the hopelessly idealized tribal woman he has invented to make Daisy think of him as not entirely innocent: she comes to possess the imaginative force of a symbol in his mind, representing, as he becomes increasingly battered and disillusioned by his urban experiences, the possibility of a meaningful existence and fulfilment within the tribal framework. It is to Abrahams' credit that for all the faults of this novel, and the persistent tendency to sentimentalize, he steadfastly rejects false optimism or easy solutions for either of his main characters.

The heroine is Myra Van der Merwe, the English wife of the Minister of Native Affairs. Her struggle to win her husband's support for South Africa's entry to the war functions on a symbolic level in the same way as Dick's urbanization: it is an emblematic rendition of a historic process at work in South African society. The chapter which describes Van der Merwe's return to his home and rural constituency to discover 'the will of the (white) people' on the issue is entitled 'The Good Bourgeois', which makes it clear that Abrahams regards the deceit and final defeat, both political and personal, that Van der Merwe suffers to be inevitable. Although the line is quite drastically modified, Abrahams' reading of the South African situation is fundamentally a Marxist one at this stage, and he sees no

---

[1] *Ibid.*, p. 177.

18

place for well-intentioned, honest whites; and though one would hesitate to call Van der Merwe a 'liberal' in any sense, Abrahams excludes liberalism from any possibility of relevance to the situation through his treatment of Solomon Ashe, the liberal professor. The latter, together with Dr Timbata, the old-school African leader and the 'best' bourgeois in the book, is depicted at one stage as suggesting, prophetically, a Bantustan-style solution for the racial crisis to Van der Merwe in the latter's ministerial office!

Van der Merwe held out his hand. Ashe shook it. Then he turned to Timbata. He held out his hand again.

'How d'you do, Doctor ... I've just been looking at your book. Rather late, I must confess ... Please sit down.'

They sat down. Van der Merwe pushed a box of cigarettes forward. 'What can I do for you, gentlemen?'

Ashe looked at Timbata. Timbata cleared his voice:

'We have a plan which we hope you would consider and express your opinion on.'

'Yes?' Van der Merwe thought, what a clear deep voice the man has.

'This plan sprang from a desire, very natural in an African and also understandable in the friends of the Africans, to effect a greater degree of freedom both socially, politically and economically for the Africans. As it is quite obvious that both the European section and the Government are opposed to granting equal rights to the Africans, or even granting certain rights, we have a plan for complete, absolute segregation, politically and otherwise. The plans are complete.' Timbata opened his case and pulled out a volume of bound, typewritten sheets. He handed it to Van der Merwe. He continued: 'What it boils down to is this: we suggest that the Government make a grant of a certain sum of money and set aside certain tracts of land either in the Transkei or up North in the Pietersburg area, and permit, let us say a hundred thousand Africans to settle there and build up a self-supporting group. This group will owe allegiance to the Government, but will run its own domestic affairs. It will set up its own factories, shops; have its own police and courts, and its own Government.

'This would solve what is known as the Native question without any disruption of the country. Even as an experiment it should be worth-while trying because for affairs to go on as they are doing is disastrous. Sooner or later there will be friction.'

'Such a State—for we might call it that—will need a good amount of trade to be self-supporting,' Van der Merwe said.

'Yes. If the Government had a group of trained technicians to help the colony in the initial stages and also to train Africans to take complete charge, that would do it.'

'You don't see my point, Doctor, producing goods is one thing, the important thing is to get a buyer for your products.' Van der Merwe mused, then he looked up at Timbata and smiled. 'And besides, Doctor, it looks to me as though it would be a case of jumping from the frying pan into the fire . . . . You'll be setting yourself up in competition against the European producers.'

'It's not a case of competing,' Ashe broke in, 'this seems to be the only way of solving this very vexed problem. It isn't right that one group should be so dominated by another, no matter what the reason, and surely, if association is odious or undesirable, then development along parallel lines is the best and most desirable thing.'[1]

What makes it clear that the ideas expressed by Timbata and Ashe are unacceptable is Timbata's conservatism, his rejection of the younger generation of radical politicians emerging within his own movement. There is no real presentation of the arguments involved on this issue: just a dramatized interpretation of what Abrahams believed was really going on in South African society. His vision of contemporary political history emerges from the parallel strands of Dick's experiences and Myra Van der Merwe's choice. Together they render the values of bourgeois liberalism invalid in the area which they define. Myra's decision to leave her husband and return to England when the latter, a victim of political pressure and deceit, declares his opposition to the war with Germany in parliament, corresponds

[1] *Ibid.*, pp. 39–40.

with Dick's decision to return to Johannesburg after he realizes that his visit home has not been the experience of spiritual regeneration he had hoped for. They have both been betrayed by the weakness of liberalism, by the impotence of the well-intentioned bourgeoisie: Ashe and Timbata, instead of campaigning for entry to the racist war, divert themselves with irrelevant and defeatist proposals to solve a problem that is, to say the least, not separate from the need to defeat Nazism; while Van der Merwe betrays Dick as well as his wife, because he is Minister of Native Affairs and ultimately responsible, politically at least, for what happens to Dick both in town and at home in the countryside. Myra's departure is the symbolic divorce between the values of English liberalism and white South Africa.

These are the twin inevitabilities of the situation in South Africa, as Abrahams saw it—the urbanization of Nduli and the divorce from English liberalism. And who can deny that he achieved a measure of prophetic insight? The condemnation of the 'good bourgeois' is equally perceptive in the light of subsequent history. For all the book's gaucherie and stylistic ham-handedness, Dick emerges (though he is presented strictly from the outside) as dignified, if not convincing as a human being: a solemn and upright puppet who is never quite ridiculous; while the feeling of tenderness between Myra and her husband, overwritten as it is, somehow strikes among all the discords a genuine note; and Myra's feelings when she decides she must leave her husband and return to beleaguered England and the values he has forsworn, are genuine and moving. In the change in Dick's sensibilities and the disintegration of the Van der Merwes' marriage Abrahams can be said to have transcended the immaturities of style and perspective, in his partial success in the crucial novelistic enterprise of presenting credibly the notion of change as a process linked by time to events in individual human lives.

But the failures and shortcomings are serious enough and in general, unfortunately, they foreshadow weaknesses that persist. The attempt to create structural links and parallels between the two major strands fails through sheer improbability. When

Van der Merwe goes home, on the visit already mentioned, he discovers that Uys, his gigantic idiot cousin, has given one of the African farm-girls a child. Van der Merwe buys her off with a large sum of conscience money (not that she is 'on' to anything) and sends her home to her tribe. When Dick goes back to his kraal at the end of the book, the reader discovers that the woman is his sister. So he and Van der Merwe have a blood relation in common: but no other contact whatsoever. The irony is too neat, the probability too remote, the coincidence too perfect. The respective returns to their rural roots by Dick and Van der Merwe are intentional parallels: the results contrast, only too neatly, at all major points. Van der Merwe goes back to find out something about others, allows others to dictate his choice, makes the wrong one and returns to confirm his error and lose his love. Dick returns to complete an inner quest, makes his discovery for himself, and choses to return to the city on the basis of what he has discovered; there is no hint that he has lost Daisy and his choice is represented as not only inevitable but positive—and, what is more, hopeful. (Abrahams' optimism at this point must either be seen as long-term or mistaken.) Van der Merwe returns to face the end of something of value; for Dick, the return is a new beginning, fraught with symbolic possibilities:

It was night when the train pulled into Park Station. Dick got off and went out of the station. Everywhere little lights glimmered. Brilliant lights of many colours. He remembered the first time he had seen Johannesburg. He had topped a hill and as he looked down he had seen it. A vast sea of twinkling lights, as far as the eye could see. Lights everywhere, like stars on the earth. And from the starlit earth he had heard a low hum drifting up to him. That was the song of the city. He listened for it now. Yes, there it was. Deep and low and monotonous. Telling the tale of the hearts of all its children. Tales of laughter and tears; of loves and hates; of death and of life.

He walked on and Mnandi was there again. Warm and soft and inviting. And she was singing. And her song was lost in the song of the city. And words ran through his mind, keeping union with his footsteps:

Oh sing then the song of the city,
Sing it when your heart is in pain,
For you are a son of the city
And the song will lighten your pain;
To-day there is pain—but to-morrow
The song will be gay—rich with hope.[1]

The most disastrous section of the novel, and that which embodies Abrahams' most persistent and damaging weaknesses as a novelist, is the one that deals with the Ashe family and especially the younger daughter Naomi. She spends a night and a day away from the stifling security of her home, among a group of new-made friends: Ernst Cellier, an unbelievably cynical and boozy young journalist who wears symbolically thick glasses; his girlfriend Lee, a painter: Roger Jones, a communist trade unionist who works among non-whites, and, though very briefly, Van der Merwe's brother Wilhelm, the Nazi editor of an Afrikaans daily newspaper. (The prophetic touch becomes uncanny here: the unlamented Verwoerd was convicted as editor of an Afrikaans daily during the war for disseminating Nazi propaganda: he later became minister of Native Affairs, before becoming Prime Minister.) The only interest provided by this level of the plot lies in a conversation between Naomi, the sensitive but innocent budding liberal, and Roger the dedicated communist, which indicates the grounds of Abrahams' personal rejection of Marxist ideology and the values he adopted in preference:

'You like your work, don't you?' She watched the tired eyes.
'I don't know: It's work that has to be done, it's important, and I know I have to do it. You might call that liking it, I don't know, but it's more a question of first things first. And for me this is first. I think I would like more than anything else to be a teacher in an ordinary school because I like children and I like to teach them. As a matter of fact, I was a teacher for a little while. But this comes first, so there's no question of liking or disliking.'

---

[1] *Ibid.,* p. 179.

They walked on. Naomi toyed with the thought that had come into her mind.

'You know,' she said slowly, 'it's harder to understand you than it is to understand either Lee or Ernst. I think it's because everything you say comes from your head and not from your heart. There's always something to it. Something planned that leads in a very definite direction. I thought you were angry when you spoke to Ernst, when you quoted that verse, but you were leading in a definite political direction again. Don't you sometimes long for the language of the heart? Not to be going anywhere but just to be drifting?' Again she watched the tired eyes and wished to know what feeling was behind them. She said: 'There must be a point of human contact with you somewhere.'

'Isn't this walk a point of human contact?'

'Don't you feel lonely sometimes?'

He smiled and lit a fresh cigarette. He lowered his head and stared at the pavement. He blew out a cloud of smoke and said: 'I feel lonely for many things, but what good is that? Ernst felt lonely for many things and tried to set them right in his own way. Now he's lonelier. So lonely that he verges on madness. His loneliness grew inward and threatens to destroy him. Even if I do escape my loneliness where can I run to?'

'The companionship of people with whom you have things in common.'

'And that is?'

'People you can love and share things with. Books, pictures, meals, laughter, and even your pain.'

'And what if I have no money for books and pictures and meals?'

'You can work for it.'

'I grow old sometime, and then what? You saw those natives this afternoon. Every single one of them wants a point of human contact, but they get it in the colour bar. Man is more than just a pleasure-seeking thing. He's a creative animal, and it's only just that he should enjoy the fruits of what he makes. My point of human contact is with those people who are alive and building for the future.'

'But what do you want out of life?'

He smiled and turned his tired eyes to her; a faint light of mockery shone from his eyes: 'Tell me, what do you want out of life?'

She thought for a moment, then said: 'I want peace and friendship and freedom, and as many of the good things of life as possible. I want to travel and do things of that sort.'

'What do you think the ordinary native girl wants out of life?' he asked.

'Pretty much the same things,' she said.

'What do you think the Jewish girl in Germany wants?'

'Isn't that too simple?' She smiled at him.

Naomi slowed her steps as they neared the house. It was good to walk with Roger in spite of his staid inflexibility. So nice and so honest. She liked him and wanted to tell him so. But she knew it wouldn't mean anything.[1]

Admittedly the contrast is based on stereotypes and the level of the dialogue not exactly sophisticated: but Abrahams at least presents the alternatives. Politically, in this novel, it is clear that he regards Roger Jones as standing for something more worthwhile than the Ashe family: but he also perceives a missing dimension in Jones' outlook, and it is a dimension that is to become crucial in Abrahams' later work: that of the individual in relation to the possibilities and pitfalls of personal freedom. Significantly, his friendly antagonist, Naomi, is also his ally, in that her commitment to individuality complements his stern dedication to the People: also, she rejects her father's stuffy and theoretical academic liberalism in favour of an ethic to be discovered through living.

Apart from this, there is no doubt that the novel would have benefited greatly from an almost complete excision of all material relating to the Ashe family and their friends. The lesson that Abrahams had not yet learnt was that you can't communicate everything at once: that is why the novel is at the same time short and uneconomical. In fact, he had less to say than he thought he had, though what was worth saying was far from valueless.

[1] *Ibid.*, pp. 105–6.

2

Mine Boy

Mine Boy must be considered Peter Abrahams' first substantial novel. It was published in 1946, under the imprint of Dorothy Crisp; it was reissued in 1954 by Faber, after the double success of *Return to Goli* and *Tell Freedom*; and it made its inevitable appearance in Heinemann's African Writers Series in 1964. It contains an element of the inevitable also in its constitution, in relation to Abrahams' development. His need to express exhaustively the various meanings held for him by the experience of life in Johannesburg had been manifested clearly and frequently in his short stories and in *Song of the City*, and for the South African writer rendering the unusual point of view of the black man in white society, the urban situation presented the archetypal challenge.

Mine Boy represents, perhaps, a more disciplined and less diffuse attempt to meet this challenge than *Song of the City*, and yet in overall terms it is arguably less successful. By selecting two aspects of urban life, each of them a matter of economic necessity, and sticking to them, Abrahams is able to present a more easily graspable pattern of experience within an ideological framework that is relatively clearly defined while avoiding the diversity of episode and resultant weaknesses of plot that mar *Song of the City*. On the other hand, the worlds of the African mineworker and the shebeen queen possess relatively little elasticity, and the temptation to reduce character to wooden stereotype within a predictable plot structure is often overwhelming.

To say that the ideological framework that encompasses the novel is a limiting factor would not necessarily imply an adverse criticism, since the canons of social realism make no allowance for the criteria of bourgeois aesthetics. This is to say that *Mine Boy* is a proletarian novel whose plot displays a Marxist perspective on life. It is proletarian in the sense that it is about members of the working class and consciously stresses the idea that the conflicts and difficulties of the Africans in town life in South Africa have their basis in the class struggle. It contends that the problems of white workers are fundamentally similar. The two groups share a common interest; when they recognize this and act together they will overcome their problems.

This was the party line on South Africa for a long time, and Abrahams' acceptance of it is unsurprising in relation to his political development. The book was written during the war, at a time when his association with communists in England was close, and direct experience of South Africa fresh in his mind.

William Empson's well-known essay suggests that proletarian equals modern pastoral,[1] and certainly elements of Empson's argument are borne out by Abrahams' performance in *Mine Boy*. The hero, Xuma, is a highly representative figure, coming raw from the country to seek work on the goldmines in the big city. He undergoes a transformation in the course of the novel, from being the embodiment of everything that is rural in location and traditional in morals, to the new man, hero and leader of the new class: but his successful growth depends on the health of his former roots.

Xuma as a character is defined by his experiences in the city. These are intimately connected with the inhabitants of a house in Malay Camp (an old, slum area of Johannesburg once populated by Africans, Coloureds and Indians) which doubles as a shebeen (a sort of saloon bar where liquor is sold under illegal conditions). Until 1962 it was a criminal offence in South Africa to sell alcoholic beverages of almost any kind—except traditionally prepared beers, and those only under rigorously specified monopolistic circumstances—

---

[1] *Some Versions of Pastoral* (Peregrine, England, 1966), chapter 1.

to non-whites. As a result the practice of illicit liquor selling flourished, especially in the towns, where it became institutionalized in various forms. The inhabitants of the house include Leah, the shebeen-keeper; Daddy, an elderly and incontinent drunkard; Ma Plank, Leah's older assistant; Eliza, Leah's adopted foundling who has become a schoolteacher; and Maisy, a winsome urban lass. The household revolves around Leah, predictably enough, since she is perhaps the archetypal Abrahams dominant female, motherly, powerful, decisive, fearless, protective, sexual and wise. She is frequently imitated, if never surpassed, in the later novels. She takes in the helpless Xuma, who is lost, hungry and cold on the night of his arrival in the city from the north.

If Xuma represents the rural life at the beginning of the book, Leah embodies all the learning that the city has to teach, and the polarity that quickly emerges between town and country is first manifested through their relationship. She is soon telling him (in order to avoid misunderstandings):

> I am here, you see, I come from my people, but I am no longer of my people. It is so in this city and I have been here many years. And the city makes you strange to the ways of your people, you see?[1]

But he doesn't really understand and the more extended, allegorical explanation given by Daddy at Leah's behest similarly fails:

> 'The custom and the city,' he murmured, then his eyes lighted up and he smiled. 'The custom and the city, ah. Very funny. Just you listen . . . .'
>
> He got up and walked up and down the room. He rubbed his hands, smiled knowingly and smacked his lips. He lifted first one shoulder then the other.
>
> 'Very funny,' he said. 'One day the city came to visit the custom, Xuma. And the custom was kind. It gave the city food and it gave the city beer and it gave the city beautiful young women . . . .'

---

[1] *Mine Boy* (Heinemann Educational Books, London, 1963), p. 23.

'No, Daddy,' Leah interrupted.

'Quiet, woman!' Daddy said very firmly.

Leah smiled.

'. . . As I was saying, it gave the city beautiful young women. And then what do you think? Unbelievable. The city didn't say a word. It didn't say "No thank you" and it didn't say "thank you." And the people said, "Ah, everything will be all right now, the custom and the city are friends." Hmmmm . . . They did say that and they went out into the fields to look after their crops. And when the sun was going down they came back and looked for their beer but their beer was gone. And then they looked for the custom but he had gone too. And the city was there laughing at them. And now they go to jail if they drink beer. That's why I like beer . . . Very funny, heh, Xuma? Well, that is it and I want to go to sleep . . .'[1]

This passage is intended to give the reader a wider view of the situation rather than to influence the raw young Xuma. He is soon at moral odds with Leah over her refusal to share the information she buys about the liquor squad's interest in the doings of the shebeen queens with any of her colleagues in the trade:

'You will not tell the others,' (the policeman) said.

'I look after myself,' she replied and turned away.

The policeman rode away.

'Come,' Leah said and led the way back to the house.

Xuma caught up with her and took her arm.

'Will you tell the others?'

'What is it to you?' she said pulling away.

'You are a strange woman.'

'You are a fool! . . . Come! I have much to do.'

. . . Leah went out and shut the door behind her.

Then she pushed her head back into the room again. 'Xuma, I'm not angry with you but don't be such a fool. If I tell the others the police will know we have been warned and that will be no good . . .'[2]

---

[1] *Ibid.*, pp. 24–5.
[2] *Ibid.*, pp. 39–40.

It is clear that Xuma's country code is meant to embody, in however naïve a manner, virtues like loyalty whose application may seem universal but which are rejected by even the kindly and good in the city. The relevance of his values has to be proved afresh, but this can only happen after they have developed and been modified through participation in urban life.

This plan of action is rigorously executed by the author, within the limits of his ability. It follows from these requirements that every episode Xuma encounters, every relationship he makes, must in some way exemplify an aspect of city life, so that he will be able to accumulate experience by contact with it. The plot is exceedingly episodic, but far from the liveliness and vigour of the picaresque. Most of the small episodes, cameos encapsulated in the texture, thrust in by the brutal syringe of coincidence, have to do with violence, and Xuma's response to violence establishes the purity of his moral sense. His friends find his reactions inappropriate and embarrassing. This separates him from their passive if resentful acceptance of the exigencies life presents for the black townsman.

On the first of these occasions, during his first afternoon in the town, he goes for a walk in the streets of Malay Camp under the direction of Joseph, the brother of Leah's man. This is an opportunity for Abrahams to attempt to present a vision of the city through Xuma's unaccustomed eyes, but the result is rather confused. It is heavily authorial, saturated with information that Xuma could not have had time to acquire, and decidedly weak through its very lack of specificity in the evocation of atmosphere. But the standard description of the African working class disporting itself on a Saturday afternoon comes to an abrupt and significant climax.

A Coloured man and a very pale woman passed Xuma and Joseph.

'Look at those black fools,' the woman said.

The man laughed.

Xuma felt a pang of shame and turned to Joseph.

'They are the fashion makers,' Joseph said.

'But it is foolish.'

Joseph looked at him and said nothing.

Suddenly a Pick-up Van swerved round a corner. Policemen jumped out and ran down the street. The crowd scattered.

'Come!' Joseph said.

People ran in all directions. The gamblers made a grab for the stakes and ran ... Only the Coloured people did not run.

'Come!' Joseph urged again.

'But we have done nothing.'

'They will not ask you,' Joseph said in disgust and dashed down the street.

A policeman was only ten yards away and he was coming straight at Xuma. Xuma waited. He had done nothing. He had just stood there watching. The policeman came nearer. He raised his stick and brought it down with force. It missed Xuma's head and struck his left shoulder. Pain shot through his body.

'I have done nothing,' he said and grabbed the policeman's arm before he could hit again.

'Let go! Bastard!' the policeman shouted and kicked out.

Xuma felt pain shooting up his leg.

'Dog!' he whispered and struck the policeman in the face. A look of strange surprise crept into the policeman's eyes. Xuma trembled with anger. He bunched his great fist and struck again. Hard. The policeman groaned and collapsed in a heap and lay still.

Xuma looked around. The van was still a distance away but two policemen were closing in on him.

'Now I will run,' he said and ran down the street.

'Stop that man,' one of the police shouted.

A Coloured man stepped into the road and held up his hands. Xuma braced himself. His heart was pounding but he ran easily. He must be careful or this yellow bastard would deliver him to the police.

Another Coloured man stepped into the road. Xuma felt afraid. To run and knock down two men at the same time was impossible. They would catch him. He could hear the feet of the policemen behind him. He hated the Coloureds. He would hurt one of them before they got him. These half-castes!

An unbelievable thing happened. The second Coloured man knocked the first one down and ran down the street waving to Xuma.

> Xuma smiled, and increased his pace.
>
> 'Thank you, brown man,' Xuma said.
>
> 'This way,' the man said and swerved into a passage, 'we will lose them.'
>
> Xuma followed him.[1]

Whatever the deficiencies of narrative technique, the implausible convenience of the episode's position in time, one cannot deny a certain skill of economy that evidences itself in the actual presentation. Every little internal event or perception tells: it has its weight in the rhetorical structure; and this fits precisely with Abrahams' strategy. He is, after all, concerned with a kind of propaganda—information conducive to the establishment of particular conclusions. And in this he is successful. Xuma's resistance to the policeman occasions surprise in the latter. The point is taken that resistance is an unusual response in the circumstances. The divided behaviour of the two Coloured men illustrates the contradictory situation of their entire community, and Xuma's reactions to them suggest his greenness as well as the black stereotype of the Coloured people. Xuma's closeness to the rural tradition is suggested by the simplicity of his thoughts and words, and the ceremonious courtesy with which he thanks his deliverer. The most important underlying rhetorical point is also conveyed strongly: the necessity and effectiveness of concerted action and solidarity between all oppressed people in the face of the oppressor. The level at which this is effective is allegorical rather than symbolic: at this stage Xuma is the innocent hero, natural man in his unfallen state. But he is so little related to his new reality that after his escape from the policeman he cannot find his way home again:

> Xuma had found the street without trouble. But it was difficult to find the house. The houses all looked the same in the gathering twilight. The same verandahs. The same yard gates. The same corrugated iron walls leaning drunkenly backwards. And all the same dirty colour.[2]

---

[1] *Ibid.*, pp. 30–32.

[2] *Ibid.*, p. 34.

As well as Xuma's fundamental displacement the passage suggests that depersonalization and lack of individuality are a condition of non-white urban life. This suggestion is taken up and elaborated into a full-scale dramatization of the Marxist theory of alienation in the description of Xuma's work on the mines. The passage stands in its own right and is convincing and horrifying.

> With another he had pushed the loaded truck up the incline. The path was narrow on which they had to walk and it was difficult to balance well. And the white man had shouted, 'Hurry up!' And the induna had taken up the shout. And one little truck after another, loaded with fine wet white sand, was pushed up the incline to where a new mine-dump was being born.
>
> But as fast as they moved the sand, so fast did the pile grow. A truck load would go and another would come from the bowels of the earth. And another would go and another would come. And another. And yet another. So it went on all day long. On and on and on and on.
>
> And men gasped for breath and their eyes turned red and beads of sweat stood on their foreheads and the muscles in their arms hardened with pain as they fought the pile of fine wet sand.
>
> But the sand remained the same. A truck would come from the heart of the earth. A truck would go up to build the mine-dump. Another would come. Another would go ... All day long ...
>
> And for all their sweating and hard breathing and for the redness of their eyes and the emptiness of their stare there would be nothing to show. In the morning the pile had been so big. Now it was the same. And the mine-dump did not seem to grow either.
>
> It was this that frightened Xuma. This seeing of nothing for a man's work. This mocking of a man by the sand that was always wet and warm; by the mine-dump that would not grow; by the hard eyes of the white man who told them to hurry up.
>
> It made him feel desperate and anxious. He worked feverishly. Straining his strength behind the loaded truck and running behind the empty truck and looking careful to see if the dump had grown any bigger, and watching the sand from the earth to see if it had grown less. But it was the same. The same all the time. No change.

Only the startling and terrifying noises around. And the whistles blowing. And the hissing and the explosions from the bowels of the earth. And these things beat against his brain till his eyes reddened like the eyes of the other men![1]

The analysis of the psychological consequences of this degrading form of work is expressed through Xuma's own reaction, and his implied frame of reference is again his rural background, where one worked for direct benefits, both tangible and intangible. Depersonalization and reduction of the individual to a unit in the managers' calculations come into this, but the virtue of Abrahams' description lies in convincing us of the effects of the experience on Xuma in terms of neurotic behaviour. Because the reduction of a human being to the level of a 'sheep' (Xuma says the eyes of the other miners 'are like the eyes of sheep') is a process; it begins with the realization of how pointless one's work is. This realization is stronger and more demoralizing in the long run if a point of contrast exists. For Xuma (and presumably the other mineworkers) this lies it their own rural experience. Other obvious aspects of the mineworkers' lives, such as racial prejudice, exploitation, an irresponsible attitude towards safety on the part of the managerial group, are all touched upon. Abrahams' initial emphasis on alienation is not only his most original and profound contribution to an outsider's understanding of the experience, it is also most effective. The evocation of Xuma's growing sense of anxiety and psychic unrest as the nature of his work fails to compensate for the battering his senses undergo from the continual noise, explosions and whistle-blasts of his strange new environment amounts to a fine piece of psychological realism.

One reason why this passage stands out is the predictable nature of the remaining treatment of Xuma's work. Xuma becomes a boss boy, working underground, endowed with considerable responsibility for the safety and work performance of the gangers under him. Together with Paddy, his white foreman, he elicits compensation from the reluctant

---

[1] *Ibid.*, pp. 65–6.

management for one of the miners who has been stricken with pneumoconiosis (miner's phthisis), which used to be the scourge of South African mineworkers: he draws attention to a fault in the wooden struts in one section of the mine, and disagrees with the engineer's diagnosis of its safety. Later, the collapse of these supports leads to the book's climax.

The political aim of the book is realized through standardized events of this kind, in which the relationships between characters who represent larger and conflicting interests are confined within a pre-determining ideological framework. But the description of the effect of the work on Xuma's sensibilities succeeds on a different and more meaningful level because in it Xuma exists simultaneously and convincingly as an individual as well as a representative of a class. He is not merely the stock hero of stock goldmining situations but a man in a universal situation whose reactions to specific aspects of it acquire universal significance.

The theme of alienation is broadened by embracing victims whose symptoms are not directly related to work, but to the general racial set-up. Three of these stand out: Daddy, a nameless African doctor, and Eliza, Xuma's teacher girlfriend. Daddy, as has been mentioned, is a hopeless alcoholic wreck of a man who lives at Leah's house: yet he embodies, with an effort, the version of wisdom which narrates for Xuma the parable of the custom and the city. Even at critical moments, such as the solemn council Leah holds to try to find out who is betraying her liquor-selling activities to the police, Daddy is able to do no more than lean 'against Ma Plank, his mouth half-open, a drunken film over his eyes'.[1] In general Abrahams' treatment of him is gauche to the extent of patronage. Daddy is a rigid stereotype, a scarcely credible character, a jerky puppet laden with the idea of folk wisdom corrupted by urban degradation. This makes his life story even more difficult to accept, the contrast scarcely falling short of the grotesque when we learn that

[1] *Ibid.*, p. 186.

'. . . when he first came to the city he was a man. Such a man! He was strong and he was feared and he was respected. And now you scorn him. You may think I am an old woman but I tell you, Xuma, he was a man such as I have never seen.'[1]

The narrator is Ma Plank, who goes on to tell how

'. . . when there was trouble about the passes he stood at the head of the people and he spoke to hundreds of them and the police feared him.

'He understood and he fought for his people but he understood too much and it made him unhappy and he became like Eliza. Only he fought. And listen, Xuma, that one lying there in his own piss is wiser than Eliza. He can read and write even better than she can. He found Leah in the street and looked after her. . . .'[2]

Daddy dies because he has been knocked down by a car. After an intensely melodramatic deathbed scene, when he describes the funeral Abrahams penetrates the layer of sentimentality that covers too much of the surface of the novel.

At the head of Daddy's grave they put a little cross with a number. And under the number they wrote his name. Daddy was called Francis Ndabula . . .

For a time people would mourn Daddy, and then they would forget him and the mention of his name would grow rare. Another old man would ultimately become the drunk old man of the street. Maybe they would call him Daddy too. And the Daddy who was Francis Ndabula would be forgotten. Only those of his own house would remember him. And even for them the memory would grow faint and misty. Life is so . . .[3]

In this way the contrast between the two Daddies is given perspective and significance. Understanding dawns with clarity

---

[1] *Ibid.*, pp. 115–16.

[2] *Ibid.*, p. 116.

[3] *Ibid.*, p. 200.

of the extent to which urban life for the African in South Africa is fundamentally a process of depersonalization, of stripping the individual of his identity and reducing him to membership of a menial group. Even within the confines of this group personal identity is problematical—even for his closest companions Daddy's real name has disappeared. The suggestion seems to be that there is no escape for the black man from the crippling virus of racist exploitation that pervades the urban environment. At first there is a retreat from the complete and depersonalized slavery of the work world into the meagre protection of a group of fellow-oppressed, within which a sort of half-man may be permitted to emerge. The fullness of being is suggested only in death, which is too late.

Thus this passage is closely linked with the earlier description of work alienation, and both have their structural origin in the description of city life—'the custom and the city'—Daddy gives Xuma at the beginning of the book. It is ironically fitting that the cause of Daddy's death—the motor accident—is peculiarly urban.

The final comment 'Life is so . . .' is meant to convey a sense of defeat, a fatalistic attitude induced in the mourners by the unremitting hostility of their environment and their living conditions and experiences. It is thus not intended to suggest a fundamental acceptance of basic processes or conditions of reality that are intrinsically inescapable, such as the rhythm of birth and death. Abrahams' lack of deftness in merging his point of view with that of the group of mourners gives rise to the possibility of confusion.

This quality of fatalistic acceptance of defeat is also prominent in Xuma's first encounter with the black doctor. They meet one evening in a crowd of people watching police in a rooftop chase after a man who has been playing dice in the street. The man falls, and the doctor intervenes.

> Then the man moved. The crowd became individuals again. The doctor ran forward and knelt beside the man. The crowd pressed close around.

'Give him air,' the doctor said.

Xuma pushed the crowd back. 'Give him air,' he repeated. The doctor felt the man's body all over.

'It's all right, only his arm is broken.'

The doctor looked at Xuma.

'Help me get away,' the man whispered.

Suddenly the crowd pushed and moved back. Policemen pushed through.

'Stand back,' the foremost shouted.

Xuma moved back with the crowd. Only the doctor remained.

'You!' the policeman said to the doctor. 'Didn't you hear?'

The doctor got up and looked at the policeman.

'I'm Doctor Mini.'

The policeman laughed. Another behind him pushed forward and smacked the doctor in the face. Xuma bunched his fist and took a deep breath.

'You'll hear about this,' the doctor said.

The second policeman raised his hand.

'You'd better not,' another policeman said and stepped forward. 'He is a doctor.'

The other two looked at the older policeman. There was disbelief in their eyes.

'It's true,' the older policeman said.

'I want to take this man with me,' the doctor said, looking at the older policeman. 'His arm is badly broken and he's got to be looked after.'

'No bloody fear,' the first policeman said. 'He's going where he belongs, in jail.'

The doctor took out a card and gave it to the older policeman. 'I'm attached to the General Hospital, and this is my home address if you want me. I'm taking this man with me. You can come and get him in an hour's time. And when you come I want to lodge a charge against this man for assaulting me!'[1]

Xuma helps the injured man to the doctor's car and goes with them to his home, where he finds the same sort of middle class

---

[1] *Ibid.*, pp. 104–5.

domestic comfort he has just seen in the flat of his white overseer, whom he had met by coincidence in the central part of
town earlier during the evening. Dr Mini and his wife receive
him kindly and understand his bewilderment. He feels ill at
ease, as he had felt in his foreman's apartment: 'As though he
did not belong there and it was wrong for him to be there.'
But the doctor explains:

> '. . . You are not copying the white man when you live in a place
> like this. This is the sort of place a man should live in because
> it is good for him. Whether he is white or black does not matter.
> A place like this is good for him. It is the other places that are
> the white people's. The places they make you live in.'[1]

Just then the doctor's nurse comes in excitedly to tell him
that the patient has escaped through the window.

> Xuma watched the doctor's face. For a minute there was sadness
> and hopelessness in it. Like the faces of the men who had worked
> on the pile of fine, wet, white sand that would not grow less.
> It was there for a minute, then it was gone, and his face was
> again cold and calm and hard to make out.[2]

The doctor dismisses Xuma brusquely, and he feels hurt:
but his wife behaves more graciously.

> He turned abruptly and walked to the door. The doctor's wife
> followed him. She held out her hand and smiled at him.
> 'Thank you very much,' she said.
> Xuma took her hand. It was soft and small like the white
> woman's.[3]

The white woman in question is Di, the girlfriend of Paddy,
Xuma's Irish foreman. Xuma has met them earlier in the same
evening during a lively stroll through Johannesburg streets,
savouring from afar the forbidden delights of the white man's
existence. They had invited him to Paddy's apartment, where

---

[1] *Ibid.*, p. 109.

[2] *Ibid.*, pp. 109–10.

[3] *Ibid.*, p. 110.

39

he had eaten with them, ill at ease: she had tried to persuade Xuma of the irrelevance of colour as a barrier between human beings, but the going is hard. Afterwards she holds a colloquy with her boyfriend, who is significantly nicknamed 'Red', not only because of the colour of his hair, on the subject of Xuma; it is remarkable mainly for its confusion. Di contends that Xuma is 'not a human being yet' because, unlike Eliza, he has not reached the stage of resentment: 'She's a social animal; he's not.' Paddy exhorts her to 'for God's sake have faith in human beings. It is not enough to destroy, you must build as well. Build up a stock of faith in your breast in native Xuma, mine boy, who has no social conscience, who cannot read or write and cannot understand his girl wanting what you want.'[1]

Doctor Mini makes one more appearance, when he stands helplessly at Daddy's deathbed. Abrahams' view of him carries a trace of doctrine: the doctor mirrors, and embodies, the impotence and guilt of the middle class African, politically isolated from the mass of the oppressed workers, and yet a part of them by virtue of his colour and his rejection at the hands of the white community. In relation to his own group it is scarcely surprising that his response to his work resembles that of the black miners: and this identity of response to work is the author's way of showing that Doctor Mini and Johannes the miner are in the same political boat.

The most complex and least successful study in alienation is Eliza, the teacher with whom Xuma falls in love. Her portrayal is mainly unsuccessful because of the very peculiar and consistent manner in which Abrahams falls victim to a version of feminine mystique in all his attempts at female characters. Thus Eliza's idiosyncracies—her veering moods, fits of guilt and remorse, alternating bouts of acceptance and rejection of Xuma, culminating in her sudden and secret departure from the scene —*may* all be the effects of the corruption of her potential. This corruption is caused by the resentment thrust upon her by

---

[1] *Ibid.*, p. 101.

her racial position as an educated African woman in South African society. As she puts it after rejecting Xuma in bed:

> 'I am no good and I cannot help myself. It will be right if you hate me. You should beat me. But inside me there is something wrong. And it is because I want the things of the white people. I want to be like the white people and go where they go and do the things they do and I am black. I cannot help it. Inside I am not black and I do not want to be a black person. I want to be like they are, you understand, Xuma. It is no good but I cannot help it. It is just so. And it is that that makes me hurt you . . . Please understand.'[1]

Her alienation takes the form of a crisis of identity. She cannot allow her attraction for Xuma to reach whatever degree of fulfilment is attainable precisely because of the unnatural limitations on this fulfilment that exist. She cannot identify her destiny with Xuma's obvious traditional virtues of strength, honesty and purity of mind because she has been seduced into seeing them as relative to the equally obvious virtues of the achievements of the white society which surround her but are denied to her.

Unfortunately all this is somewhat vitiated by the fact that almost all Abrahams' female characters behave in the same 'typically feminine' way as Eliza, being capricious, indecisive, moody, and dangling their men on a string. All they lack is the intellectual awareness Eliza has of her problem of identity.

Still, she is a phase in the process of Xuma's personal development. An inner conflict takes place between his passion for Eliza and his liking for Maisy: he only grows out of the one and brings the other to realization at the very end of the book. Both are, of course, representative figures within the propaganda framework. Maisy, whose hand, unlike Eliza's, Di's or Mrs Mini's, is work-hardened, stands for the real quality of black city life, without fundamental convictions and without pretensions; whereas Eliza is a torn product of the unborn future, a

---

[1] *Ibid.*, p. 89.

destructive half-born child, yearning for the inevitable reality to come.

After Xuma and Eliza consummate their bliss and enter on their brief and remarkably conventional domestic idyll, the plot, such as it has been, becomes alarmingly episodic. In very short order the reader is presented with the murder of Dladla, a violent friend of Leah's who has been betraying her business activities to the police: Leah's subsequent arrest on suspicion and release, Daddy's fatal accident and death (after which Xuma is entirely surrounded by women—Leah, Eliza, Maisy, Ma Plant, Lena—a characteristic situation for one of Abrahams' heroes), Eliza's sudden departure, Leah's capture in the act of concealing liquor and her sentence of nine months' imprisonment. As she is taken away by the police she makes an almost authorial apology, to the reader as much as to Xuma: '. . . I am sorry everything happens together . . . Life is so always.'[1]

Leah's arrest brings Xuma's psychic crisis to a head; the urban conditions of life seem to triumph over the purity of his spirit, and he constitutes a classic case of severe alienation:

> Since that Saturday night when Leah had walked down the street with policemen flanking her, all feeling had left Xuma. Only a tiredness remained. A tiredness and many questions that were a strain on his brain for he could find no answer to them. And sleeping, too, was hard, for the tiredness of the body had to fight the restlessness of the mind. It was as though the real Xuma was dead and only a shell remained. There was feeling, but it was like the feeling of a stranger, for it did not hurt. He did not feel pain any more. There was no lump in his throat. His heart did not beat violently. He could smile easily. He did all the ordinary things he had learnt to do since he came to the city. Everything seemed just as it had been. But it was as though another person looked at them and did them and thought about them. Something was lost. Something that had been there all the time, inside him. It was not there now.[2]

---

[1] *Ibid.*, p. 229.   [2] *Ibid.*, p. 232

Ma Plank and Maisy come to see him, to housekeep and to try to 'cheer' him.

> He had wished they would not come to his room but it had been too much trouble to ask them, so he had left them and they had come. They had tried to speak but there was nothing to say. Then, after a time, they had stopped coming. The last time Maisy had been to his room she had stood at the door and said, 'When you want me, come to my work place. Ma Plank is there with me. We will be happy to see you.' Then she had gone. Many days ago that had been . . .[1]

By this time Xuma has 'become a citizen of Malay Camp'. He is recognized and greeted in the street by his fellow inhabitants, who know of his troubles, 'for in a strange manner that no one knows the people of Vrededorp and Malay Camp get to know about everybody else.'

He goes to visit the house in which had slept his first night in the city, Leah's house, and finds strangers living in it. He imagines he sees it filled with his old companions, but 'suddenly the illusion had faded'. The reader is presented with the realization that for Xuma, Leah's house and her circle had been a transitional stage between rural tradition and urban barbarity. Leah and Daddy had their roots in the past, too. The blow had been cushioned for him by the false security afforded by the house and its inhabitants; he is now at last face to face with the complete grim truth of city life.

It is at moments like this one (there are not enough of them, however) that the novel really functions in the way a proletarian novel should. The central character (who unavoidably belongs to a different class from that of the reader) is presented to the reader as possessing an inner reality much like his own, as feeling and suffering in the same ways for reasons which emerge to attain concrete and specific substance in relation to the genuineness of the hero's emotional life. The hero becomes an individual, shedding the grey garb of 'the worker' or 'the

---

[1] *Ibid.*, pp. 232–3.

miner' or 'the black man', and his circumstances become real in proportion to his individuality, instead of the mere evocation, however powerful or tiresome, of a propaganda litany. The reader is made to understand that a working man's working life *is* harsh and dull and unpleasant, that his home circumstances aggravate rather than alleviate the overall effect of depression this has, and that the *results* in terms of feeling, of emotion, of psychological state, are recognizable to the reader because he has, for whatever reasons, experienced them himself, if not to the same degree. In short, the main propaganda function of the proletarian novel is to transform the worker into a suffering (in the broadest sense) human being; and this is where it co-incides with its purpose as a work of literature.

Perhaps it is true that the nature of such a work makes moments like these rare and elusive: it is certainly the case that this level is not maintained through the climax of the book, which comes immediately after. It begins with a lengthy conversation between Paddy and Xuma early one morning as they go off night shift. Paddy tries to urge Xuma out of his depression, telling him he must fight against it: not, as Xuma objects, with bare hands against guns:

> '. . . There is another way.'
> 'What is it?'
> 'You must find it, Zuma. Out of your feeling and out of your pain it must come. Others have found it. You can too. But first you must think and not be afraid of your thoughts. And if you have questions and you look around you will find those who will answer them. But first you must know what you are going to fight and why and what you want.'
> 'Why do you, a white man, talk to me like this?'
> 'Because first, Zuma, I am a man like you, and afterwards I am a white man. I have seen the sickness of your mind. I work with you every day and I saw your sickness and I understood.'[1]

This provokes Xuma into being unusually articulate:

---

[1] *Ibid*, p. 235.

'You say you understand,' Xuma said, 'but how can you? You are a white man. You do not carry a pass. You do not know how it feels to be stopped by a policeman in the street. You go where you like. You do not know how it feels when they say "Get out! White people only." Did your woman leave you because she is mad with wanting the same things the white man has? Did you know Leah? Did you love her? Do you know how it feels to see her go to jail for nine months? Do you know Leah's house? Did Leah take you in in the middle of the night?' Xuma's voice rose. 'Did Leah talk to you and laugh with you from the side of her mouth? You say you understand. Did you *feel* these things like I do? How can you understand, white man! You understand with your head. I understand with pain. With the pain of my heart. That is understanding. The understanding of the heart and the pain of understanding, not just the head and lips. I feel things! You want me to be your friend. How can I be your friend when your people do this to me and my people?'[1].

And he concludes: 'I am a black man. My people are black. I love them.' But Paddy, the Red One, is equal to Xuma's outburst.

'That is good. It is good to love one's people and not to be ashamed of what one is. But it is not good to think only as a black man or only as a white man. The white people in this country think only as white people and that is why they do this harm to your people.'
'Then I must think as a black man.'
'No. You must think as a man first. You must be a man first and then a black man. And if it is so you will understand as a black man and also as a white man. That is the right way, Zuma. When you understand that you will be a man with freedom inside your breast. It is only those who are free inside who can help free those around them.'[2]

Xuma's outburst to Paddy has the effect of getting rid of the immature egocentricity that has clouded his perceptions (though

[1] *Ibid.*, pp. 236–7.
[2] *Ibid.*, p. 237.

of course to be fair, the mechanics of the plot do seem to conspire to produce the feeling that everything happens to *him*), and leaves a clear field for new impressions and ideas. Paddy seizes the chance of making Xuma see himself as a social being, part of a broader social organism whose functioning can be explained, understood and altered. But Xuma does not have much time to ponder the implications of his new vision. The following night he arrives at work to find that there has been a collapse in the underground workings, and his friend Johannes is trapped with Chris, his white foreman, Paddy's friend. Xuma and Paddy go down, against the mine manager's advice, and come up bearing the bodies of their friends. The engineers arrive and find that the props had collapsed at a place where Xuma had previously warned of danger. The manager and the engineers conclude that Chris and Johannes, foreman and boss boy,

> '. . . lost their lives through panic.'
> Paddy grabbed the man and felled him with one blow.
> 'They looked after their men,' he said. 'We warned you about that thing a long time ago.'[1]

Xuma emerges as an individual and refuses to take his men down on shift until the supports are repaired. Paddy is caught indecisively in the middle. The manager calls the police; striking is prohibited for non-white workers in South Africa.

> 'Come on, Paddy!' a white man called. 'It's all very well to play with them sometimes but we must show these kaffirs where they belong. Come on!'
> This is what I argued with Di about, Paddy thought. This is the test of all my verbal beliefs. Zuma has taken the leadership, I must follow. Di was wrong about him. He's a man.
> In the distance they could hear the siren of the police cars. Soon now the police would be here. Paddy walked over to Xuma and took his hand.
> 'I am a man first, Zuma,' he said.[2]

---

[1] *Ibid.*, p. 247.   [2] *Ibid.*, p. 248.

He goes on to call on the black miners to refuse to go down, and Xuma 'smiled. Now he understood. He understood many things. One can be a person first. A man first and then a black man or a white man . . .'[1]

The police arrive to arrest Xuma and Paddy. A mêlée breaks out and Xuma, after knocking two policemen down, makes his escape, somewhat improbably, on foot to the house in the suburbs to tell Maisy that he loves her. His emergence to full manhood has at the same time resolved the Eliza-Maisy conflict: his love for Maisy is a reflection of his maturity. Then Maisy accompanies him on his way back to give himself up to the police, because he says he cannot forsake 'the Red One', and

> '. . . there are many things I want to say too. I want to tell them how I feel, and how the black people feel . . . It is good that a black man should tell the white people how we feel. And also, a black man must tell the black people how they feel and what they want. These things I must do, then I will feel like a man. You understand?' He looked at Maisy.[2]

Maisy understands.

Perhaps the obvious comparison for *Mine Boy* is William Plomer's *Ula Masondo*, his short novel (or long story) about a Zulu tribesman who goes to work on the mines in Johannesburg.[3] *Mine Boy* displays nothing of Plomer's elegance, economy or wit, and in some respects Plomer seems closer to an adequate awareness of urban African life than Abrahams. But there are two important distinctions to be made: first, significantly, in Plomer's story the final word is left to an outsider, a white storekeeper who once sold the hero a blanket. Abrahams uses no such technique of letting the facts and the mistaken judgments speak for themselves, whether ironically

---

[1] *Ibid.*, p. 249.   [2] *Ibid.*, p. 251.

[3] Mphahlele draws the comparison in *African Image* (Faber and Faber, London, 1962), p. 177.

or directly. His purpose differs from Plomer's, being more directly political, and he attempts to remain steadfastly within the black world with all its inarticulacies and bewilderments when it comes to making judgments. Secondly, and the two points are connected, Plomer's work belongs to that large genre which charts the corruption of the innocent tribesman by the city's wiles and temptations. It is not relevant to object that Plomer's sympathy is clearly with the victim. Abrahams refuses to accept the stereotype of the black man as victim, and Xuma differs from Ula and all his literary fellow-fallen in that he finds his true strength and being in the city. Thus he is in the end conscious of the price he has paid and must go on paying, simply to retain his integrity as a black man and a worker in a white bourgeois world. This consciousness is an important extension of the realm of possibility for the newly-urbanized African.

After the woodenness of characterization, the improbability of diction, the failure to create a convincing matrix of work experience (a serious drawback in a novel of this kind) and unevenness of plot have all been duly noted and condemned, *Mine Boy* remains an important novel, even in some ways a powerful one. Its power is derived from the imaginativeness of the undertaking and the originality and scope of the underlying idea, which turns the literary stereotype of the inevitable corruption of the innocent black man by the white city on its head.

3

The Path of Thunder

It is apparently quite obligatory for all South African novelists to try their hand at least once at the theme of miscegenation. The frequency of attempt at the topic is matched by the high proportion of failure. There are several reasons for this. Usually a writer of one culture describes a relationship between a member of his, dominant, culture and someone from a subservient group, and generally the author has neither the factual material nor the sympathetic insight to render the personality of the alien character satisfactorily. Often such works are exercises in self-fulfilling prophecy: they are written with the intention of demonstrating the inevitable failure of long-term sexual relationships across the colour line. The intention may be artistically permissible—just; but since it is always executed through the prejudices of the writer, which are identical with those of the dominant group (to which he belongs), the demonstration turns out invariably to be a particularly dishonest form of special pleading. Objectivity and detachment or any degree of aesthetic distance are qualities virtually absent from this class of novel, even in those which go against the prejudices of white South African society. The result is that the emphasis is seldom on the aspect of personal relationships that it pretends to be (and that would be the most satisfactory from a novelist's point of view), but rather on a state of affairs, constituted by a particular set of relationships between groups, which is what the writer is usually more interested in than in the individual characters, who are as a result concocted of the familiar ingredients of stereotype.

The rhetoric employed by most of the South African writers of novels on this theme is depressingly uniform and predictable. The white men who transgress this most fundamental commandment of their group's racial purity, are at the very best psychological cripples, victims of severe neurosis like Coenraed de Buys in Sarah Gertrude Millin's *King of the Bastards*; more usually, they begin with a fatal flaw in their characters, they are born with the seeds of degradation in them. They are seldom the victims of circumstances alone. Like Mrs Millin's Rev. Andrew Flood in *God's Step-children*, they are clearly physically repulsive and morally weak. Their female partners in degeneracy may possess a degree of physical attraction at the outset: by the end, or long before, they go fat and ugly and toothless and syphilitic. They are harridans whose only intelligence takes the form of low cunning. They never emerge as characters.

One of Abrahams' original contributions to this literary sub-species was to reverse the sexual roles, as it were. In this he was preceded only by William Plomer, whose *Turbott Wolfe* (1924) was not really about miscegenation as such. The central characters of *The Path of Thunder* are a Coloured man and a white woman, which in itself suggests how precisely opposed Abrahams' basic assumptions and purposes are in this novel to those which had been almost universally accepted by his white predecessors. In Sarah Gertrude Millin's *The Dark River*, John Oliver, the central character, is irrevocably repudiated by his wife, when she discovers that years previously he had lived with a dark woman and had begotten children of her, with the words: 'If I had lived for eleven years with a drunken Kaffir—'.[1] Her husband finds this unanswerable because of the implied reversal of sexual roles, and their relationship disintegrates. And George Findlay points out that up to 1927 the only form of sexual relations between members of different colour groups that was outlawed in all four provinces of the Union of South Africa was that in which

[1] S. G. Millin, *The Dark River* (Collins, London, 1920) p. 219.

the *female* partner was *white*.[1] Only in Plomer's *Turbott Wolfe*, had this sanction been flouted before: and two more different works than Plomer's elegant and eloquent satire and Abrahams' impassioned treatise are hard to imagine, though ultimately their goals converge.

It should be explained that since 1927 all forms of sexual relationship between members of different racial groups have been prohibited by law in South Africa. The necessary legislation was passed by a parliament composed only of white members, representing for all practical purposes the wishes of only white constituents. Thus the plot of any South African miscegenation novel has an immediate and precise politicolegal frame of reference.

The Path of Thunder is concerned with the fate of Lanny Swartz, Coloured schoolteacher, who, on graduating from the university, returns from the intellectual stimulation and comparative social freedom of Cape Town to the poverty and backwardness of isolated Stilleveld, the highveld Coloured village where he was born, in order to set up a school and improve the lives of his people; and Sarie Villier, member of the Boer farming family which dominates the area. Each is attracted to the other by the unusual qualities which distinguish them from the other members of their respective racial groups. They soon fall in love, and the outcome of their relationship, as Abrahams takes pains to emphasize, is as inevitable as it is tragic.

In most of the earlier novels about miscegenation, the intention was to dwell on the weakness and folly of some rare individuals, in an otherwise reasonable and normal universe. In Plomer, Abrahams and most of his successors—notably Jacobson—the intention has been to establish the fate of reasonable and normal behaviour on the part of rare and isolated individuals acting in a universe pervaded with hostility

---

[1] G. Findlay, *Miscegenation: a study of the biological sources of inheritance of the South African European population* (The Pretoria News and Printing Works Ltd, Pretoria, 1936), pp. 5–6.

and irrational evil, and peopled by more or less willing agents and victims of these negative forces.

The Path of Thunder was Abrahams' third novel (though it was his fourth published in Britain, a year after *Wild Conquest*, while it had first seen the light in the United States as much as four years previously, in 1948). It relies heavily on early materials and memories of the author's South African experiences, and at the same time betrays a distance growing increasingly difficult to bridge between the remembered perception of the real situation and the fictive interpretation of it. There is thus little that is fresh or vital about the book: it is impassioned and highly subjective, a fierce cry for elementary justice in a crude fictive framework. It constitutes the uneasy climax to Abrahams' first phase of development. Between it and *Wild Conquest* there is a world of difference, of careful thought and studied detachment.

In a way these remarks tend to undermine the novel's main virtues which are precisely those of passion, of energy, of commitment, of a direct belief in humanity and civilized values. The trouble is twofold: even though the form of commitment is comparatively new and very outspoken in relation to the situation in the South African novel at that time, in broader terms Abrahams has nothing new to say; and then there is the way he says it, which time and again turns out to be particularly unfortunate. Abrahams is far from being in full control of his material. This is illustrated best by his weakness for those two associated phenomena so frequent in his work, violence and sentimentality. It is perfectly true that the situation described is the most pregnant with violence of any possible South African plot; and it can be argued that at best the massive dose present in *The Path of Thunder* constitutes a kind of emblematic rendition of the condition of the whole society. The violence begins, in fact, with the Kaffir Wars, which the old grandmother living in decrepit exile in a corner of the Villier farm because she knows Gert Villier's guilty secret, still relives in her senile hallucinations: and it persists in the Villier family's relationship with their Coloured peons. Years before the action of the plot Gert

Villier has kicked the head in of a young and handsome Coloured man from Stilleveld who had won the affections of the woman Gert wished to marry. The Coloured man survives the attack disfigured and subject to fits of madness. He is called Mad Sam, and is symbolic of the relationship between white and non-white in South Africa. But Mad Sam is also Lanny's forerunner, a prefiguration of the inevitable fate that must befall Lanny and Sarie.

Lanny's first direct encounter with violence takes place significantly early, in fact immediately on his arrival at Stilleveld:

> Across the way from the siding was a little coffee stall. A buxom Afrikaner lass tended it. A lorry stood a little way from the stall. Two bronze, muscular men were drinking coffee. They all looked at Lanny. . . .
>
> —'Do you see what I see?' one of the men asked.
>
> The other pursed his lips and looked doubtful:
>
> 'I'm not sure. It looks like an ape in a better Sunday suit than I have but today's not Sunday so I'm not sure.'
>
> 'Perhaps he wears suits like that every day. . . . Besides, you are all wrong, he's too pale to be an ape. That's a city bushy.'—
>
> Lanny reached down to pick up his cases. The best thing he could do was to get out of here. There was no sense in looking for trouble. He'd take any one of them, but of course they wouldn't fight fair.
>
> 'Hey! You!'
>
> Lanny stretched himself and waited. He had discussed the colour question a lot in the National Liberation League and the Non-European United Front and now it had picked him out. It had called him.
>
> 'Come here!' It was the first man.
>
> South Africa, Lanny thought tiredly, this is South Africa. He walked across the narrow track. At least they won't frighten this Coloured, he decided; hurt me, yes, but frighten me, no. He stopped directly in front of the man and looked straight into his face.
>
> The man inspected him closely.
>
> 'Where you from?' the man shot at him.

'Cape Town.'

'What do you want here?'

'I live here.'

'Haven't seen you around.'

'I've been in Cape Town for seven years.'

'School?'

'Yes.'

'University?'

'Yes.'

'What are you?'

'What do you mean?'

'I mean what I say. Have you any fancy titles?'

Lanny smiled. 'Yes. I have two.'

Suddenly the man's hand shot out and cracked across Lanny's mouth. With an effort Lanny controlled the instinctive urge to strike back. The man saw the move and struck again. Lanny touched his lips with his tongue and spat. A patch of red blood dropped on the fine dust and seeped through it. Lanny watched it.

'Don't smile at me!' the man hissed.

South Africa, Lanny thought, this is South Africa. And this man in front of him resented him because he was educated and showed independence. If he had been humble the man probably would have been kind to him, smiled and sent him away. This was still the old struggle for conquest. The history of his country. This man in front of him had to dominate him, he was fearful in case he did not. This was the history of South Africa in stark, brutal reality. He saw it clearly suddenly. Not out of books. Not with kindly lecturers talking and eager or indifferent students making notes. Not these. No . . .

For a while the man's eyes rested on the fountain pen in his pocket.

'Education,' the man said bitterly.

And still Lanny saw the battle going on. Zulu impis against white Voortrekkers. The bitterness of that fight. The native fighting for his land. The white man fighting for a foothold and fighting even harder to retain it.

In a few seconds the turbulent history of the country rolled over his head like a huge wave and was gone. He shuddered as the wave passed . . .

'Well?. . . .' the man threatened.

Lanny knew that all he had to do was to lower his eyes or look away—any gesture of defeat would have done—and the man would tell him to go.

He returned the man's stare. The man raised his fist.

I will not give in, Lanny decided, and turned and walked away.

'Bastard!' the man roared.

A pang of fear gripped Lanny's heart but he kept on.

'No! Don't!' It was the girl.

Lanny picked up his cases and walked along the sandy track. This was the road home. Soon now he would get there. Soon now he would hear the simple Afrikaans of the old folk. Soon now he would see Mabel. Yes, this was the road home. His head throbbed painfully. This was the road home. He bit his lips and held his head high. He stepped onto the grass as the lorry went past. Something wet struck his cheek. He wiped the spittle away . . .[1]

The processes of Lanny's thought during this encounter (one or two paragraphs of it have been omitted here because of their repetitiveness) carry a heavy burden of solemn historicism, material which Abrahams might have contrived to have presented to the readers' awareness in another way, as it is extremely unlikely that a character faced with the threat of a thorough and unpleasant beating would allow his reflections to stray so far from the paths of self-preservation. The situation may indeed represent 'the history of South Africa in stark, brutal reality . . . Not with kindly lecturers talking and eager or indifferent students making notes'; but it is an aesthetic disaster that Lanny's thoughts are allowed to wander in such academic woods at the time—and at such enormous length!

There is a good deal of this kind of inappropriateness, this straying between inner and outer life, in the book, stemming largely from the fact that Abrahams had, in a sense, too much

---

[1] *The Path of Thunder* (Faber and Faber, London, 1952), pp. 18–21.

to say, and was not skilful enough technically to integrate it with the action to an even remotely satisfactory degree. This failure is even more glaring, and more of a flaw, in a novel in which the events of the plot are confined within a deterministic framework. The events thus become instruments of a remorseless machine or process of action; but they are so feathered by verbiage that the reader scarcely sees their operation as a process.

In terms of the theme of violence the progression of the novel may be said to consist in the development of Lanny's courage and defiance: courage in the face of threatened and actual violence, defiance of the accepted pattern of the Coloured man's response to his white oppressors. On the night of his arrival—the same day on which the encounter already quoted takes place—he is summoned by Gert Villier to the 'big house'.

> Lanny remained standing near the door. The big man at the table did not move or look up for what seemed ages to Lanny. He sat like a statue carved in human flesh, motionless and impersonal. Neither a positive nor a negative force seemed to flow from him. Like somebody dead, a deep recess of Lanny's mind whispered. Quiet settled over the room. Lanny fancied he could hear the thumping of his heart. And in fancy the thumping grew louder. His body began to tremble. He felt painfully tense.
>
> This is what he wants, Lanny told himself. He shook off the oppressive feeling and looked at the man at the table. It's all right, he told himself, I won't let him dominate me and I won't speak first. He called me: let him speak.[1]

Villier does eventually break the silence, going into a violent tirade which concludes with the words: 'We do not like independent bastards here, *Mister* Swartz.' Lanny is ambushed by two whites as he leaves the farmhouse, but hits back 'instinctively'—an important word—before going down: he is saved from further maltreatment by the advent of Sarie, whom Lanny

---

[1] *Ibid.*, p. 64.

had encountered for the first time much earlier during the same eventful evening.

This instinctive retaliation is meant to separate Lanny from the majority of the Coloured men of Stilleveld, or of anywhere else in rural South Africa, from the man

> late for work (who) hurried out of a shack at the lower end of the High Street and trotted away praying that the white man would not sack him. That he would be abused and probably kicked he expected . . . There was a young one coming in a few weeks and the wife had to have something.[1]

Lanny is intended to be a hero, but here again the machinery creaks ominously. His heroism is related clearly and inescapably to that which differentiates him from the others : his possession of education. Lanny is the only educated Coloured man in the book, apart from Mad Sam. Apart from Mad Sam, he is the only one who retaliates when attacked, who stands on his humanity when confronted by forces that endeavour to negate it. Abrahams seems to be stressing a point of somewhat dubious validity, when he insists on education as the key necessity for initial liberation and self-realization. He is well enough aware that often for the individual non-white this conflict with white society begins to assume its full complexity with the acquisition of 'white' education, and he specifically rejects the error of seeing education as a solution to anything. He thus denies what in other places in the book and elsewhere he seems clearly to affirm—the Romantic idea of the potential greatness of the human soul—by his insistence on making that greatness not only potential but conditional on the possession of a particular tool, the acquisition of which is a matter of intelligence or even luck rather than character.

So a connection exists between education, or at least the ability to communicate in the white man's terms, to use the skills of the dominant culture, and the ability to defy the power

---

[1] *Ibid.*, p. 181.

structure on which that culture rests. This may appear to be a statement of the obvious, but in fact we are dealing with a rather special case. Lanny has only one kind of goal open to him— that of the romantic individualist who seeks fulfilment as a self-sufficient being in relation to society. But he is by definition an outcast from the particular society whose goals he adopts and prefers. White South African society as it is depicted in the novel has no reference to reality unless it is seen as a version— indeed, the only available version—of European culture, offering the goals and aspirations characteristically generated by that culture to its members. It is a distorted version, a twisted idea: Lanny is doomed to come into conflict with it because he has been taken in by the pure source. (The number of times he, or Mako, or Sarie, or Finkelberg quote from the early Romantic poets may be regarded as an indication of this.) It is this assertion of the pure idea against a deformed but dominant version of it that gives rise to the clashes, which are all expressed in terms of physical violence, and through which Lanny's heroism is defined. This is really the first time in a novel by Abrahams that the standard Western novelistic concepts of heroism and fulfilment are whole-heartedly adopted: there is no serious attempt in *The Path of Thunder* to advance the Marxist jargon of the earlier urban proletarian novels. Even Mako, the intellectual African schoolteacher who comes nearest to the role of political guru in the book, recognizes the passage from Shelley which Lanny unconsciously quotes, and which forms one of the book's superscriptions. He goes on immediately to define the form the standard goal must take in the circumstances: "'It was an Englishman called Shelley," Mako said. "He loved freedom and fought for it. If he had been alive today he would have fought for the freedom of the African people."'[1]

Freedom is political freedom: the spirit must seek first that kingdom in order to reach a stage from which it is worthwhile, or even possible, to aspire further. And this goal is necessarily

[1] *Ibid.*, p. 94.

involved with violence, as Mako makes clear. Shelley would have 'fought for the freedom of the African people.' Mako goes on: '"It want to like other people too, but how can I like those who are hard on my people? I must fight them. And when we are free, then I will learn to love them."'[1] Thus a kind of dialectic *is* present. At this stage the only form of fulfilment open to Lanny is the fulfilment of violence. Hence the inevitability of his death, and the nature of it. It is a prefiguration of the coming mass struggle for freedom, which will be motivated by love or, as Mako suggests, the desire for love. So Lanny's heroism is that of the man who has failed in his honourable and necessary quest for a goal that is rendered unattainable by historic circumstance. He is the tragic hero, doomed from the outset.

So the novel is an interesting mixture from the point of view of Abrahams' development. In it he chooses for the first time to adopt without equivocation the liberal-humanist values and goals that are universal characteristics of the novel form: but he subjects these values to a dialectical framework, with the intention of demonstrating that however desirable they may be, they are 'historically' incapable of being realized, and that true heroism consists in trying to break out of the dialectic, and going to the ultimate in the attempt. The book thus stands in precise transition between the early work and the later, between acceptance of Marxist values and philosophic ideals and those of Western liberalism. Its position is denoted by the author's use of violence as a means of marking the hero's progress within the dialectic.

But the trouble lies in Abrahams' weakness as a craftsman. This is strikingly illustrated by the affinity between violence and sentimentality that exists not only in *The Path of Thunder* but in all his work. If we define sentimentality as an aberration from literary realism, characterized by a preference for unlikely symmetries in relationships and events in a form which is basically unsympathetic to this kind of symmetry, leading to a

[1] *Ibid.*, p. 95.

degradation in the characters and feelings portrayed, it becomes clear that it is a phenomenon likely to be associated with 'closed-ended' works, those in which a predetermined ending is only too apparently foisted on the characters from the start. (This is not to argue that all Aristotelian tragedy is sentimental. Obviously, the two forms require—and evoke—different types of suspension of disbelief.)

The sense of inevitability that is such an insistent aura surrounding the fate of Lanny Swartz is most forcefully expressed by Finkelberg, the young Jewish intellectual would-be author (an unconvincing portrayal, to say the least). He and Mako meet at the same time as Lanny and Sarie have their assignation after an interval of painful restraint on Lanny's part. Finkelberg says:

> 'There's something like inevitability about the way they seem drawn to each other. They don't seem to be able to control their feelings.'

Mako is sceptical, but Finkelberg goes on:

> 'You don't understand, Mako. There are two ways of falling in love ... You and I know one way. You look at a woman. She has a pretty face and figure, her legs are just the right shape, the way she carries her head, the way she looks at you, the way she speaks, all these things you admire and what you see urges you to fall in love with her. And then, perhaps, you find that you like the same things, enjoy doing the same things, and think the same things are important; if it is so then your love develops and grows. That's one way. That's the love we understand.
>
> 'But there is another kind too. By that love people are just drawn together without looks or anything else mattering, not even the fact that this is the highveld.'
>
> 'I don't believe it, Finkelberg.'
>
> 'Yesterday I would have said the same, Mako.'
>
> 'Swartz must be a fool. Why didn't he go away?'
>
> 'You're asking why a drowning man struggles for his life.'
>
> 'This fatal, inevitable love is nonsense.'
>
> 'For you, Mako, yes. But not for Swartz. I don't know what it is. I know the fact that your internal freedom is greater than

his has something to do with it. You are at once freer as well as being more restricted because you have a past and a tradition whereas he has none——'[1]

More accurately, Lanny is being denied his birthright since he is the illegitimate son of old Gert Villier, though he doesn't know it: and as we have indicated, Abrahams makes it clear to which tradition, intellectually and spiritually, Lanny cleaves. It is in this respect that he is a symbolic figure. He is representative of the Coloured people's dilemma. In a situation in which whatever cultural or moral tradition that is available and worth having comes from the white group, which is a parent group in every sense, the Coloureds are specifically excluded from participation in this tradition by that very group, except on the basis of a rigid adherence to a minutely-defined pattern of subservience. The fate of anyone who defies this situation is inevitable. Two Coloured characters in *The Path of Thunder* defy it. They are Mad Sam and Lanny, and they are both doomed men. Mad Sam's fate is a fairly precise prefiguration of Lanny's, up to a point, as Gert reveals just before the moment of climax:

> Gert brought his face close to Lanny's. He could see the pain in those eyes.
> 'I'm not going to kill you,' Gert said. 'No. I'm not going to kill you. I'm going to squeeze more. Squeeze till you are weak and then I'm going to kick you. Do you hear, *Mister* Swartz?'
> Lanny was helpless. He could feel great drums beating in his ears.
> 'Yes,' Gert gloated. 'I'm going to kick you and kick you until you are like Sam. They call him Mad Sam. But he was like you. Thought he was good enough for a white woman. Just like you, educated and well dressed and with a clever tongue, and I made him what he is today. My slave! He was stronger than you! *I* kicked him and now he moves like an animal. That's what's going to happen to you, *Mister* Swartz!'[2]

But Mad Sam himself intervenes, and he and Gert kill each other. He had loved another Sarie, who had been destined to

---

[1] *Ibid.*, pp. 162–3. [2] *Ibid.*, p. 258.

be Gert's wife. His feelings had been reciprocated, but Gert's destruction of his humanity had also destroyed the woman they both loved. By this time, very close to the end of the story, Lanny is aware of all this. And this penultimate scene of violence leads swiftly into the climax, in which Lanny and Sarie barricade themselves with guns into the Villier homestead and shoot it out with Gert's henchmen, the local whites, killing three before succumbing themselves. The final burst of violence is a symbolic climax, however redolent of inferior Western film technique it may be. It is symbolic because in it Lanny has a gun, the ultimate defiance, the final assumption of equality with the white man in South African society. And Lanny's assertion of his manhood is tragically complete as he turns that gun on white men. The final image is, incidentally, a curiously white South African one, of the beleaguered minority fighting outnumbered from within a fortress of some kind against the forces of negation and darkness outside, man and woman standing shoulder to shoulder in the mortal struggle to spread enlightenment. It is, ironically, a version of the laager image, with Lanny and Sarie as the trekkers, the new pioneers striking away from the limitations imposed on their freedom by a regime that is alien to the life of the spirit.

Only three male Coloured characters emerge as individuals in the novel. They are Lanny and Mad Sam, whose structural relationship is obvious, and whose symbolic functions carry one of the book's major burdens, in terms of Abrahams' notion of the fate of the Coloured people; and the preacher of the little community at Stilleveld. On one level at least this is a specific failure of opportunity, within the more general failure which is perhaps the major defeat of the book—the rendition of village life in Stilleveld. It is a strange community where men are shadows, only appearing in order to recede further into the darkness to have a furtive drink at communal welcome parties. One might have thought that from a strictly realistic point of view it would be impossible to ignore the explosive effect of an event like the return of Lanny, specifically on, say, his peer-group within the Stilleveld community. What envies, challenges, bitterness, inspiration might someone like Lanny have evoked in the breasts of the boys of his own age with whom he had grown up and had left behind to return so utterly and desirably transformed, beyond comparison with either his former self or his contemporaries' present state of existence? In fact, with just a drop of temerity one might allow oneself to suggest that the material for a much more interesting and less predictable novel could have existed if one of the untransformed boys of Stilleveld had been the hero, and Lanny merely the village teacher, his inspiration and perhaps his guide. In the event, any such Milton remains not merely mute and inglorious but invisible as well. At the very least, Abrahams' complete failure to deal with this area of relationships constitutes a lapse from realism. The reader is left with the impression that through some freak in the birth rate, Lanny was the only male member of his age group in Stilleveld, a village composed of an aged preacher, Lanny's mother, a few other assorted old women, Fieta, Mad Sam, Mabel (Lanny's sister), a handful of indeterminate middle-aged males and children.

In general the picture of Stilleveld life contains the most blatant outbreaks of sentimentality in the book. Most of the events and characters within it are straight from stock: the return of the faithful son to his mother, the daughter's escape to the big town, the simple preacher's admonitions, the village whore with a heart of gold and a tragic love that haunts her. Abrahams does much better in the closing stages of *Tell Freedom* when he describes his own youthful experiences as a teacher in a poverty-stricken Coloured hamlet on the Cape Flats. This passage describes an episode that took place just before the author made his decision to leave South Africa, and which apparently helped to launch him as a prose writer; the experience provided some of the inspiration for *The Path of Thunder*, and the descriptions of Stilleveld life quite clearly have their roots in it. It is a pity the flowers are so peculiarly synthetic and in a way insincere in their appearance. It is the same failure as that which occurs later in Abrahams' work, in *Wild Conquest* in his treatment of the Matabele, in *A Wreath for Udomo* in his description of tribal life, in *This Island Now* in the rendition of the ordinary people of the island. Of course, the difficulty is embarrassing enough to the writer at a stage in his career where he is ideologically committed to an idealization of man as a member of a socio-political group, or of that group itself—as was the case with Abrahams in his earlier works. (Though peculiarly enough this shortcoming is not as prominent in *Mine Boy* or the very early short stories; and *Song of the City* is a strangely successful early novel *except* where the author has to come to grips with the creation of some kind of homogeneous social structure with a complex set of interactions between a fairly large number of secondary characters.) From the point of view of the work itself, however, once that falls within the accepted conventions of literary realism which govern the contemporary novel in almost all its manifestations in one way or another, there are good reasons for stating that this kind of disability becomes even more of a drawback. The paradox is only superficial: the novel's essential liberalism places an emphasis on the individual such as to make the rendition of group situations of the kind defined above particularly beset with pitfalls and difficulties. Abrahams as a writer is thoroughly consistent in his faults and artistic weaknesses: he doesn't grow out of them, but they don't become worse. They affect his later work in a different way from his earlier, though, and the change begins to emerge fully in *The Path of Thunder*.

One of Abrahams' most prominent and consistent propensities as a novelist is, of course, his tendency to place the major weight of action and feeling on his women characters. In *The Path of Thunder* there are five women around Lanny, each of whom (except his mother) is as a character both more dramatic and more convincing than the hero. Mabel, his sister, (except for the disastrous—from every point of view—dream-like interlude with the honest young English anthropologist on whom she has a crush) is neatly and perceptively realized. The strains of poverty and monotony that provoke her to petty theft, rebellion against her mother and more than ordinarily intense adolescent despair are keenly felt and conveyed by the author. The last thing she needs to provoke her into running away to Cape Town is an unrequited love affair with a mysterious Anglo-Saxon academic in a motor car who feeds her dreams of escape. The purpose of the episode in relation to the novel as a vehicle for the burden of the Coloured people is quite clear, and manifests itself straightforwardly enough in Mabel's feelings as she sits in the anthropologist's motor car:

> Tentatively she touched the steering wheel and looked at him.
> 'Like it?' he asked.
> She nodded vigorously. For Mabel the world was trans-formed—she wasn't Coloured and she wasn't poor and she wasn't Mabel and she didn't work. She was a grand white lady and this was her car and this was her husband beside her. Her clothes were fine. And the world on which she looked from the little car was a beautiful fairy world. In vision things were what she wanted them to be. The cocky hardness went out of her eyes, her face softened. Wistfulness played round her mouth.[1]

But the sheer unrelatedness of it all to the concerns of the plot, the sentimental degradation Mabel as a character is made to undergo, and the utter implausibility of the situation combine to the detriment of the total presentation of the character of Lanny's sister, quite apart from the effect on the book as a whole.

> The little car moved off leaving a trail of dust in its wake.
> The hot day followed its inevitable course.
> All over the world people went about their business.
> In Cape Town.
> In Johannesburg.
> In Pretoria

---

[1] *Ibid.*, p. 105.

In South Africa.

In the continent of Africa.

And in other continents.

It was the same all over the world. People went about their business. Only it wasn't the same time all over the world. And it wasn't the same day all over the world. And people weren't all the same colour all over the world. And it wasn't a hot day like this, perhaps, all over the world. But they went about their business.

And the people of the two valleys, Stilleveld and Mako's Kraal, also went about their business.

For Mabel only, everything had ended with the going of her white man.[1]

His haste to get on to the mail boat and back to England to write a book about the Coloured people which will affirm, as he tells Fieta, that 'The Coloured people are as good as white people' places his academic flirtation with Mabel, however unconscious one may assume it to have been, in an even more unpleasant light, somehow, than if he had taken advantage of her physically. Fieta, who intervenes in their final encounter, is nonplussed by the depth of Mabel's emotion. Her eventual and characteristic solution is to slap her face in order to make her cry. Fieta is in the Abrahams pattern of a dominant and powerful yet ambivalent female character, fiercely protective of what she considers right, and deeply conservative—a sort of archetypal mother figure. She is related to Selina in *A Wreath for Udomo*, to Martha Lee in *This Island Now*, and to Leah in *Mine Boy*; her powerful first reaction to Lanny's arrival is to reject him, to tell him to go back to Cape Town and not to disturb the precarious balance of the Coloured community at Stilleveld. She is sexually attractive (again like Martha Lee and Leah), but also like them, a loser in the game of love: she has always loved Mad Sam. When Mabel has finished crying,

<hr>

[1] *Ibid.*, p. 111.

Fieta asks her:

> 'Feeling better, Mabel?'
> Mabel raised her head and looked at Fieta.
> 'You don't know how it hurts, Fieta.'
> Fieta looked away and said:
> 'I do know ... Many, many years ago, before you were born I met a man and I loved him the first day I met him. He was fine and young and strong. He was educated and there weren't many educated Coloured people in those days ... But he didn't love me. He was Coloured like me but he didn't love me, he loved a white girl. You don't know her. She died before you were born. Your mother knew her. She lived in the big house ...'
> 'Here?'
> 'Yes, Mabel, here ... He loved her and she loved him too ... The white folks nearly killed him ... He's different now and I still love him and it hurts as much to love him now. That is why I go to Cape Town and sleep with other men. I still love him ...'
> 'Sam?'
> 'Yes,' Fieta said heavily.[1]

Thus Fieta, together with Sam, fulfils a symbolic role, a challenge to the white stereotype of the fecklessly promiscuous and fertile Coloured woman; her fate is determined by what white society does to her man, ironically enough, for the sin of not loving her, but preferring a white woman. In the end Sam declares his love for her, before going out to save Lanny and kill his tormentor, Gert Villier, in the final encounter. He thus regains his manhood in two stages: the second, unfortunately (but inevitably) is death. And Fieta bears his body back to the village, followed by Isaac and Mako, the helpless witnesses, in a procession which expresses triumph as much as sorrow.

---

[1] *Ibid.*, pp. 114–15.

Claude Wauthier, in *The Literature and Thought of Modern Africa*,[1] suggests a type of character which he calls the 're-deemer', to indicate the manner in which black writers treat their white heroines who become sexually and emotionally involved with black men. 'One characteristic is common to almost all these "redeemers":' (he writes) 'like Desdemona, they come to a tragic end.' He rightly, to some extent, equates Sarie's fate with that of Lois, Michael Udomo's Hampstead mistress in *A Wreath for Udomo*, and it is true that the cha-racters are similar types. In the customary Abrahams manner, they both provide their men with emotional strength, and take a fairly dominant role in their respective relationships. Sarie is much less realistically drawn than Lois, however; her con-frontation with Celia, Lanny's Coloured girlfriend from Cape Town, for instance, is typical of stereotyped romantic fiction. On the other hand, Abrahams does succeed in suggesting, though very barely, the kind of inner conflict a choice such as Sarie's must entail. They first meet in darkness: Sarie is out walking with her dog; Lanny, on the first night of his return to Stilleveld, is sitting meditating. When Sarie discovers his identity, she is shaken by the absence of deference in his tone:

> Lanny heard a sharp intake of breath.
> 'You ... Lanny Swartz ... And you spoke to me like that!'
> 'Like what?'
> 'Like my equal ... Like a European ...'[2]

But she doesn't set her dog on him, and when he tells her that she won't because her 'nature is not completely brutalized yet', not altogether surprisingly she is taken aback and cannot even think of a suitable rebuke. The prickly Lanny proceeds:

> 'Go on! Say it. "Black bastard" is what you're looking for.'

But she is equal to this test too:

---

[1] Claude Wauthier, *The Literature and Thought of Modern Africa*, trans-lated by S. Kay (Pall Mall Press, London, 1966), p. 196.

[2] *The Path of Thunder*, p. 49.

'That's a lie! And you are a beast!'[1]

At their second encounter she saves him from a vicious assault by Gert's henchmen, and invites him into the kitchen of the homestead to tidy up.

> They walked back to the big house. Sarie gave Lanny a bowl of water and watched him wash the blood from his face. She wanted to help him dust the back of his jacket where he had lain in the sand. But something held her back. She was white and he was Coloured. It was hard, though, to remember it all the time. He didn't behave as though he were Coloured. She had to force it into her mind in order to remember it all the time.
>
> And now, should she give him a towel to wipe his face? Impulsively she gave him her own hand towel. She watched him wipe his face, then looked curiously at the towel when he returned it to her. It was so strange. He thanked her, but as a matter of course, as though he were used to getting towels from white girls, but he couldn't be—or could he?
>
> 'There's dust on the back of your jacket,' she whispered.
>
> He tried to reach it but failed. Tentatively she stepped forward and brushed it off—
>
> They smiled at each other.[2]

By his concentration on apparently insignificant physical details, Abrahams establishes at one stroke the power as well as the absurdity of the system of prejudice which affects white South Africans in their relationships with non-whites. Sarie's response to this marks her off as an individual. She is 'surprised at herself for accepting the equality that Lanny had established between them. It was unheard of. But it was even more unheard of to find a Coloured man behaving as he did.'[3]

Only Mad Sam can forget the forms of respect in addressing white people, and that is because the distortion in the relationship is located in his twisted body and disturbed behaviour. The 'normal' Coloured manifests the distortion in the way he talks to a white man. Where the body is not twisted and

---

[1] *Ibid.*, p. 49.   [3] *Ibid.*, p. 67.
[2] *Ibid.*, p. 67.

69

F

shrivelled, the spirit is: the price of manhood for a Coloured, Abrahams suggests, is as high as life itself.

Abrahams' heroes' love objects are seldom the dominant female characters in his novels; this position is almost invariably taken by the striking and often rather repulsive mother figures for whom he shows such a predilection until the most recent phase of his development. Thus Sarie fills the same position as Eliza in *Mine Boy* or Lois in *A Wreath for Udomo*, rather than that of a Leah or Selina. Her behaviour is analogous to that of Anna Jansen in *Wild Conquest*, not only in her natural tolerance and open-mindedness, but in her reliance on the emotions, on love as a guide. Sarie does not overcome her racial conflicts through a rational process such as might be provided by Mako or Tony, our English anthropologist; when Lanny tries to explain his position as a Coloured man in an abstract way she finds it difficult to understand: 'How could she understand him as a Coloured person when she knew him only as a person?'[1] Lanny stops seeing her after his sister Mabel runs away to Cape Town, out of the loyalty he feels for his mother and his fear of complications which might affect everyone in Stilleveld: eventually, however, they arrange another night-time meeting in the veld, and as Sarie waits for the hour to arrive for her to go forth, we have an insight into the way she functions emotionally:

> Why am I going to see him? she asked herself.
>
> But there was no answer. It was just the right thing to do. There was no excitement in it. Just in the same way she had gone those other nights when he did not come. And there had been no deep disappointment then. Regret, yes. But that was tempered by the knowledge that he would come. Just a warm feeling inside and an understanding too big for her to understand. And the warm feeling was there now, and the understanding.[2]

The absolute reliance on feeling in judging a difficult emotional situation is a forerunner of Anna Jansen's fierce affirma-

---

[1] *Ibid.*, p. 123. [2] *Ibid.*, p. 153.

tion to her young friend Elsie's tearful doubts about her husband's unusual behaviour towards and liberal convictions regarding the Matabele and blacks in general in *Wild Conquest*:

> 'That is important, Elsie. That is the most important. Everything that he does and says must be right if you are close to him and he holds your hand and speaks to you in a soft voice. That is important, Elsie, more important than you know . . . If his voice is soft and he holds your hand and looks into your eyes, then he can't be very wrong, Elsie. I know that.'[1]

Sarie emerges, as far as the rather attenuated treatment of her allows, as a typically romantic figure; quoting Blake, relying on her feelings, acting on impulse, piercing intuitively through deep layers of social habit and racial prejudice to the truth, which for her consists in her love for Lanny and which thrusts all other considerations aside. It is this that helps her to triumph over Celia, Lanny's Cape Town girlfriend: it is precisely Celia's rationality, her sophistication, which gives Sarie her chance of victory. Celia asks her, in their only confrontation not long before the book's gory climax, why she chose Lanny.

> 'I didn't choose him,' Sarie repeated.
> 'A woman sees a man,' Celia said bluntly. 'She likes what she sees and makes up her mind. That's what you did. That's what we all do. Later on, in the course of time we fall in love. Only cheap novelists and romantic idiots believe in love at first sight.'
> Sarie smiled. A quiet private smile.
> 'What I said is true. You may believe it or not, just as you like. Things just happen.'
> 'And what about Lanny?'
> 'It was the same,' Sarie said slowly. She was getting a little tired of the cleverness of this beautiful girl from Cape Town. 'He tried to fight it, just as I did, but it was no good. But of course, you are too wise to understand that; it's too simple, a boy and a girl meeting each other and loving.'[2]

---

[1] *Wild Conquest* (Penguin Books, England, 1966), p. 308.
[2] *The Path of Thunder*, pp. 213–14.

It is too simple to be borne by the mechanical cruelty of white South African society, with whose version of the climax of events Abrahams ends the book:

> The *Eastern Post* of the next day carried a story on its front page in bold black letters. It told how a young Coloured teacher, one Lanny Swartz, had run amok, killed a prominent farmer, Mr Gert Villier, and then been chased into the house of Mr Villier.
>
> Alone in the house was Miss Sarie Villier. He had found a gun, shot her, and then turned the gun on his pursuers. In the ensuing battle three other people had been killed before Swartz had finally been shot down.
>
> Most of the story had been told to the reporter by Mr Viljoen, assistant to the late Mr Villier. Mr Viljoen, who had led the pursuers, had received wounds in the arm and shoulder.
>
> The story ended with a strong protest against educating black people.[1]

The Path of Thunder was a difficult book to write. Nothing like it had been done before. (One cannot really consider the influence of Plomer's *Turbott Wolfe*, if any, to have been important.) Abrahams had to overcome rooted prejudices of his own, and to contend with truly formidable stereotypes in literature and in life as well as to combine a large and diverse number of different racial modes of expression into a convincing unity, without becoming reliant, where he was ignorant, on these negative stereotypes. He had to maintain consistency with characters ranging from Isaac Finkelberg and his father, to Mako. He was by no means successful in every case. Old man Finkelberg is grotesquely wooden, his son is a quasi-intellectual caricature in glasses and the unbearably stilted and pompous Mako typifies Abrahams' persistent difficulty over breathing life into his African characters—a difficulty which reaches its climax in *Wild Conquest*, the next novel to appear. The time and distance from South Africa at which the book was written do not help Abrahams to recollect emotions in tranquillity. They seem rather to have intensified his passion

---

[1] *Ibid.*, p. 262.

without correspondingly increasing his clarity of vision. The writing and the dialogue are frequently very weak, suggesting that parts of the book originated very early in his career. The device adopted to cement the parts together—the deterministic framework—is ill-suited to the open-ended form of the novel.

And yet the book carries an overall note of conviction. It almost, but not quite, hangs together on the qualities Abrahams conveys successfully: Lanny's courage, Sarie's love, the horror of Mad Sam's existence, Fieta's sorrow, Mabel's despair. Abrahams tried to do too much, and the novel is full of irrelevancies and side issues. But strong feelings sincerely conveyed compensate notably, if not quite sufficiently, for the many technical inadequacies. It is a pity he didn't tackle the theme five or six years later, when the honesty of his approach would have been more equally matched by his increased technical ability.

4

Wild Conquest

The Great Trek is the central event in South African history.
E. A. Walker, *The Great Trek*.[1]

Wild Conquest marks an important development in Abrahams'
work. It is his last substantial piece of fiction for five years,
and it represents an attempt to summarize, as it were, objec-
tively, his South African experience. He achieves the distance
necessary for impersonality by making it a historical novel,
hinging on the central event in modern South African history,
the great northward expansion of white power known as the
Great Trek.

This protracted business of covered wagons, laagers and
biltong developed out of Boer dissatisfaction with the way the
Cape was being governed by the British, and in particular the
growing influence of the liberal missionaries in the lengthy
governorship of Lord Charles Somerset (1814–26). Immediately after this period a convenient crystallization point for
Boer grievances emerged, in the emancipation of the slaves
throughout Britain's colonies (1834). This provoked, among
other things, a superb piece of self-righteous blarney in a docu-
ment called The Retief Manifesto, which every white South
African school-child has (or had) to memorize, and which runs,
partly, thus:

> 2. We complain of the severe losses which we have been forced
> to sustain by the emancipation of our slaves, and the vexatious
> laws which have been enacted respecting them . . .
> 4. We complain of the unjustifiable odium which has been
> cast upon us by interested and dishonest persons, under the
> cloak of religion, whose testimony is believed in England, to

[1] E. A. Walker, *The Great Trek* (A. & C. Black, London, 1934), p. ix.

the exclusion of all evidence in our favour; and we can foresee, as a result of this prejudice, nothing but the total ruin of our country.[1]

Abrahams wrote before the great stock-taking began which led to the current interpretation of South African history enshrined in Leonard Thompson and Monica Wilson's new *Oxford History of South Africa*.[2] He is a victim of the authorized version, and his contribution consists in his attempt to break away from this, to be impartial, to see the African side of this stirring epic. In this it should be said without delay, that he fails: but it is an interesting, even peculiar failure which had the effect of transforming his stature as an author.

As we have seen, up to this time Abrahams' fiction has been influenced more by his relationship to political attitudes and even ideologies than by interest in human beings. Problems of personality and character have been treated with facile optimism, and his books have not abounded in living characters. He has been too involved in the need to communicate his own youthful experiences in South Africa, and in *The Path of Thunder* it is clear that this vein had reached exhaustion without any new inspiration presenting itself.

The artistic necessity of breaking free from this source of material must have been clear to Abrahams, and *Wild Conquest* is an attempt to dig beneath the exhausted vein, to examine its origins, and to interpret them. Needless to say, absolute historic accuracy has been sacrificed without qualms. Mphahlele comments on this:

> Peter Abrahams has introduced a new will into past time, thus bending history to a point in order to tell more of the truth than the historian. This 'unhistorical will' operates within a short

[1] Manifesto of the emigrant farmers (English translation from Dutch original) published in the *Grahamstown Journal*, 2 February, 1837, signed: *By authority of the farmers who have quitted the colony, P. Retief. Select Constitutional Documents Illustrating South African History, 1795– 1920* (G. Routledge & Sons, London, 1928), p. 144.

[2] Vol. 1 (Oxford University Press, 1969).

space of time in history, so that the characters produced short-lived unhistorical effects . . . The author gives the unhistorical will free play.[1]

This is not relevant as a criticism of the historical novelist at work: and Abrahams is in many ways just that. He is more interested in presenting a total picture of the forces at work in a particular situation, as they act through and as they affect individuals.

Wild Conquest is divided into three sections. The first deals with the relationship between Boer farmers at the Cape and their slaves, and describes the beginning of the Greak Trek through the experiences of a Boer family, the Jansens. The second describes Matabele life north of the Vaal river prior to the arrival of the trekking Boers; and the third presents the inevitable clash between the two protagonist groups, and its outcome.

In view of his earlier position on the question of Pan-Africanism it is interesting that Abrahams clearly sees the Boers as heralds of the 'New Day' (the title of the third section of the book), and the Matabele as representative of the dying embers of a long tradition whose glory is past. Mkomozi, the wise Matabele witchdoctor, meditates on the eve of a particularly bloody feast night at Inzwinyani, the Matabele capital:

> The spirits of our ancestors are on those hills. They look down on us. And they speak. Listen, brother, listen.
>
> They tell of the past. Not the past of yesterday, but the past of long gone, the past beyond the memory of the oldest among the old, the past beyond the memory even of these ancient hills.
>
> Listen, brother! This is a night for memory. The spirits know. Have you heard of Benin? Have you heard of Ahmed Baba? Have you heard of our ancient empires and civilizations, brother? The spirits talk of them this night.
>
> Before we came down south our empires were great and great was their glory. In the city of Benin we made forms of

[1] E. Mphahlele, *African Image* (Faber and Faber, London, 1962), pp. 180–1.

beauty, in the city of Ahmed Baba we made wisdom. And then, when those empires were smashed by desert Arabs and we moved down to this southland, we built Monomatapa and we built Zimbabwe. Did you know that, brother?

But how could you? Somewhere in the ages, we lost our wisdom. Only the spirits remember and they whisper over Inzwinyani. . .[1]

The penultimate sentence is the key to Abrahams' attitude to traditional society in Africa as it is reflected in the second and third phases of his fictive development, as his allegiance to the West becomes more and more explicit. The picture of African society he gives in his description of the Matabele is one of cruelty, corruption, bloodthirstiness and arbitrary and sudden death. He relates it to a glorious and creative past.

The position of the Voortrekkers is different. Before the decisive encounter with the Matabele at Vegkop, the trek leader, Potgieter, says to his followers:

'We have come thus far. We are near the end of our journey now. Soon the long months of travel will be over. Soon we will outspan and build houses and have land. Our journey is near its end, my people . . . The land looks beautiful around here, but it is more beautiful further north. Make ready, for we leave in the morning, and the strength of the Lord goes with us.'[2]

The contrast between white confidence and black nostalgia for lost glories is deceptive, however, for it is the Voortrekker society, mainly embodied in the Jansen family, which is poisoned and corrupted by hate and the desire to destroy, while to the broken and fleeing Matabele comes a vision of the possibility of a better future in which compassion and love may flourish. Moshesh, the wise king of the Basuto, and Mkomozi, the witch-doctor, inculcate this into Dabula, the young officer who finds maturity in his people's time of defeat.

The book is a prophetic summary of the South African

---

[1] *Wild Conquest* (Penguin Books, England, 1966), p. 218.
[2] *Ibid.*, p. 298.

experience. The major group protagonists, Boer and Matabele, stand for the white and black sections of the whole population. Thus their characteristics are intended to relate to the phenomena which constitute modern South Africa. Abrahams aims at an imaginative interpretation of the relationship between past and present. In this way he is able to see right and wrong on both sides, and to assign reasons and causes for the attitudes and prejudices which define race relations in South Africa in the middle of the twentieth century. To gain this end he uses characters in each group as representatives or embodiments of various aspects of the experience of that group.

But he has a further end in view which, however trite it may sound, may also be seen as his governing obsession in writing about South Africa. This is to demonstrate that underneath their skins, whatever their differences of race or colour, human beings are fundamentally alike in their make-up. This characteristic—and very basic—humanist idea caused Abrahams, more than anything else, to deviate from his early specifically Marxist convictions and general ideological orientation, and to settle for a much more vulnerable liberal outlook—which finds its first clear manifestation in *Wild Conquest*, and dominates the second and third phases of his literary output. It is therefore natural that in *Wild Conquest* he should emphasize by contrast superficial differences, in order to stress basic similarities. Unfortunately, his imaginative range was too narrow to sustain two convincing illusions side by side, which had to bear very little superficial resemblance to each other while interpenetrating completely at a deeper level of significance.

This shortcoming is most apparent in his treatment of the Matabele. Despite the romantic passages dealing with his Elsberg childhood in *Tell Freedom*, Abrahams had little experience of 'traditional' or tribal African life. He is much dependent, as a writer, on direct personal knowledge of situations for their successful portrayal in fiction. In the sections of *Wild Conquest* which describe the Matabele, his diction grows stilted and archaic, vocabulary becomes simplified and sometimes pseudo-biblical. He encloses his Matabele in a glass case, making them seem like skilfully-mounted museum specimens who look as if they might one day—or any minute—come to life, but never do. This seriously impairs his structural technique of correspondence, that is, of relating Boer characters possessing certain traits to Matabele who are meant to be their counterparts. This occurs precisely because he is rather successful with his characterization on the Boer side, and real characters can bear no living relationship to puppets whose woodenness is the essential quality about them.

So the underlying plan of the novel is of two groups with opposing interests, in one of which the positive and life-enhancing aspects of its group morality are steadily extinguished by hate and the desire to kill, while in the other an understanding of humanist values is just beginning to awaken. The former group, being the stronger, triumphs over the latter and drives it away.

Within each of the groups a struggle goes on between characters who represent life and spiritual health, and characters who embody corruption and negation. Thus, among the Boers, it is Anna Jansen who stands for humanism, on the side of the life-giving forces: while her husband Kasper, deeply affected by the necessity of giving up his homestead and leaving it to his former slaves whom he regards as having betrayed his trust in them, becomes progressively more and more ensnared by hate and the desire to kill black people, a moral position which characterizes his brother Koos from the start.

Kasper's progressive corruption poisons his marriage to Anna. The two nights before they leave their farm 'were the only nights in all the long years of their marriage that Kasper had not been aware of her body . . .'[1] Prior to this the dormant seeds of hate in him have begun to germinate and assume their peculiar form. His brother, Koos, kills the son of the slave overseer Johannes, between whom and Kasper there had been trust and mutual respect. Kasper cannot adjust to the idea of Johannes being a free man, his equal.

---

[1] *Ibid.*, p. 48.

'What are you going to do?' Kasper asked.

'You have killed my son. If you had not done so I would have stopped him from harming you and made him give you your rifles, they were yours. But you have killed him. He has bought these rifles with his life. The life of a free man has paid for those rifles. They are ours now. You will have to kill us all before you can have them.'

'Is that all?' . . .

'Yes, that is all.'

A feeling was born in Kasper Jansen that minute. It took hold of him with the sharply painful pointedness of a needle pressed into man's most tender and sensitive organ. And like the pain in such an operation it spread to all parts of his body, to his brain and heart, to every sensitive little vein in him, it spread till it became part of him, part of the tissue and texture that went into the making of the man Kasper Jansen. That feeling was directed at the old man who stood facing him, the old man who had been his slave, the old man he felt he could trust above all the other slaves. The old man's skin was black. For Kasper Jansen the old man became a symbol for all other men with black skins. And the agency that had made it possible for the old man to stand facing him, to that, too, a share of his feeling was directed. But mainly it was directed against this old man whose face was black.[1]

Jansen is made in this way into a symbol of Boer manhood, in the same way as Johannes the slave becomes a symbol of black men to him. Abrahams stresses the depth, the almost organic quality of the colour prejudice felt by Jansen, and later extends it to almost the whole Boer community, making it a sustaining cohesive principle.

The effect this has on his marriage and his wife is totally destructive, the suggestion being that irrational hatred cannot be selective in its effects on human relations. For a long time Anna is unable to tell Kasper of her pregnancy; when she eventually does, after the Jansen family has joined a larger party of trekkers, his response defeats her attempts to make

---

[1] *Ibid.*, pp. 37–8.

contact with him. She realizes that he is being consumed by hatred, and tries to re-establish her claim on his soul.

'Kasper . . . I want to tell you something.'
'Yes?'
'I'm going to have a baby.'
'Good. When?'
'September, I think.'
Now he would say something. Now he would say he was pleased and wanted it to be another boy who would grow up to be a good Boer. Now he would come close to her again.
But he remained silent as they walked along.[1]

What distresses her most is his lack of self-knowledge, his unawareness of what is happening to him. 'Must you be hard even with me?' she asks him, and he replies 'I'm not hard.'

Anna thought: not hard. Just a Boer doing what must be done. With my Bible and my rifle. Doing what must be done. Not hard. Just doing what must be done . . . Was it wrong to want laughter and happiness? Doing what must be done. Changing to do what must be done.[2]

Anna's self-awareness is heightened and clarified after the initial confusion caused by shock, and she sees what is happening not only to the people she loves but to herself:

She leaned forward and saw the dark reflection of a willow branch in the water. Haven't seen my face since we left the valley, she thought. She bent further forward and looked into the water . . . Down there below her in the water, the outlines of a face came and went, swaying crazily one way then the next, getting squashed and short then abnormally long; eddying, billowing, shifting—the face of a woman. Suddenly, the water settled and was calm and she saw clearly. Two large eyes stared at her from a sharp, narrow face. It was the face of a stranger. Her face, the face of Anna Jansen, was round and full. She moved one hand to her cheek, and looked at the water. The face did the same. But it was the face of a stranger. How could

---

[1] *Ibid.*, p. 120. [2] *Ibid.*, p. 121.

it do the same? . . . She bent lower . . . Something caught her eyes. Hurriedly she pushed back the sleeves of her right arm and held it over the water. Yes. Yes. The arm of Anna Jansen had been round and firm and soft and strong. A lot of flesh to it. This woman's arm was like a stick. Just like a stick . . . She moved back from the water and sat up. Wonderingly, amazedly, she looked at her arm. With her left hand she touched it, feeling the flesh. There was a little just below the elbow, on the side near her body, but that was all. Everywhere else it was only skin and bone. Rough dry skin and hard bone. And my legs? She pulled up her dress. There was a hard knot at each calf. Women's thighs are always soft. Always. Quickly, she pushed her dress higher and touched the dry, thin thighs. She pushed her right hand into the top of her dress.

'I have no breasts,' she whispered . . . I am dry. Like a piece of meat that's been cut up and dried for the trek. Everything is for the trek. *Biltong* Anna. . !¹

This is an impressive passage, and Anna Jansen is one of Abrahams' best and most successful characters: indeed, she and Michael Udomo are his two most convincingly realistic characters to date. Anna's body represents the spirit of the Boer nation: her sufferings increase with time, as she sees her innocent son Stefan poisoned in his childhood by the prevailing atmosphere of hate, and hears him parrot his elders: 'I hate (the Kaffirs) . . . I want to kill many of them, like Oom Koos.'² In the circumstances Anna cannot sustain the force of life that is within her, and she dies in childbirth as the Matabele attack on the Boer laager begins. With her dying breath she calls her husband 'Killer' and he goes away to kill. Anna's simple humanism is matched by that of Paul Van As, a young and intelligent Boer to whom killing is distasteful. He fights with Koos Jansen, who has raped his girl, and though the weaker of the two, he triumphs through cunning. He learns the language of the Africans and earns the disapprobation of his fellow Boers: Anna has to reassure his young wife, drawing on her own bitter ex-

---

¹ *Ibid.*, pp. 136–7.   ² *Ibid.*, p. 302.

perience, that her husband is right and all will be well between them as long as 'his voice is soft and he holds your hand and looks into your eyes . . .'[1] Thus Anna and Paul embody a universal love ethic: Anna's vision of it is unspecific but close to the world of personal relations, while Paul's is applied essentially to the sphere of politics, or relations between groups.

But Paul's fate mirrors that of Anna: in the last battle with the Matabele he dies, leaving a pregnant wife. His final exchange is with Gubuza, the Matabele general, who is also dying: they almost discover their shared vision, but are prevented by death.

> Dying, Gubuza whispered: 'So long since I tilled the earth.'
> Paul's eyelids flickered. Elsie nursed his head. He said: 'I, too, have not tilled the earth for many months.'
> 'You understand,' Gubuza said. 'Do you all?'
> 'No. Only I.'
> 'Then you are the one who spoke to my men.'
> 'Yes.'
> 'Why?'
> 'I was for peace.'
> 'But you killed.'
> 'There is hate in my people.'
> 'I am sorry.'
> 'You are so young . . . so young to die. And by my hand.'
> 'What is your name?'
> 'Gubuza.'
> 'You are wise.'
> But Gubuza did not hear. He had ceased breathing after telling the young man his name.
> 'What did he say?' Elsie asked.
> Paul began to choke.
> 'Teach . . . our . . . child.'
> Suddenly his body relaxed.
> Elsie cried 'Paul' on a mounting note of fear.[2]

So the possibility of good, however minimal, coming out

[1] *Ibid.*, p. 308. [2] *Ibid.*, pp. 345–6.

of evil is denied. The writing is melodramatic, the juxtaposition of characters improbably neat, but the message is clear: hate is triumphant, and part of its triumph, a not inconsiderable part, consists in the deaths of Paul, Gubuza and Anna.

On the Matabele side the counterparts to Paul Van As and Anna Jansen are Gubuza, his young officer protégé Dabula, Dabula's wife Ntombi and Mkomozi the wise witchdoctor. They constitute as unlikely a quartet as one may wish to find within the pages of an historical novel. The Matabele appear frequently in novels of the Great Trek (always somewhat to their disadvantage, one feels); more frequently than the Zulu, probably because the Boers broke their military power without sustaining a major defeat at their hands. Most Great Trek novels are written from the Boer point of view, and usually they arrive at a position of 'fairness to both sides' by stressing, or suggesting, that the Matabele were barbaric but well-built, savage but more or less innocent in the sense that they were insufficiently civilized to understand the full extent of the atrocity of their actions: and that the Boers, while engaged in one of the most heroic exploits known to man, based on absolute moral propriety, *were*, after all, human too, and had their measure of lusty fellows and loose females among them.

Wild Conquest, it might be thought, begins with different assumptions from the bulk of Great Trek romances. The obvious assumption is that Abrahams might be seeking in some way to redress the balance, to demonstrate the justice of the Matabele cause, or at least to suggest the nature and magnitude of the tragedy that befalls them. Obviously, the fulfilment of such intentions depends greatly on the quality of the rendition of Matabele life and characters in the book.

Unfortunately, this is the major area of failure in the novel. To this extent at least *Wild Conquest* falls into the same category of 'fairness to both sides' as books like Stuart Cloete's *Turning Wheels* or *Fiercest Heart*, mainly because it fails to come to terms with the problem, in any new or satisfactory way, of creating convincing African characters within a given historic ambience.

84

Abrahams' knowledge of Matabele life is distinctly super-ficial, and shows no evidence in *Wild Conquest* of going deeper than, say, Cloete's, except that it avoids some of Cloete's un-healthy obsessions with the treatment apparently meted out by their comrades to Matabele soldiers badly wounded in a battle. The description of the episode which introduces the Matabele, in which the Barolong king Tauana drunkenly refuses a demand for taxation from Mzilikazi, the Matabele king and his overlord, and puts his emissaries to death, is taken almost word for word from S. T. Plaatje's earlier novel of Sechuana life, *Mhudi*[1].

Abrahams' Matabele are trick dolls who enact all the neces-sary rituals—dances, bone-throwing, smelling-out of sacrificial victims, orgies of slaughter—without disturbing the reader by the briefest flicker of life. Those whom he tries to build up into individual characters against this backdrop of group activity never emerge as more than heavily-laden vehicles for his own preoccupations. In some ways this failure is similar to that of James Ngugi in *The River Between*, as each writer felt he was faced with the same problem: the emergence of individ-uality and individuals in the Western sense from within an un-individualized group consciousness. It may well be the case that the traditional African attitude to man as an individual rather than as an organic part of a tribal or family group differs from that of Western liberals: if one may speak in such broad terms as 'traditional African'. It seems to me as likely that the Gikuyu concept of the individual may differ, or have differed, as much from that of the Matabele as, say, the liberal English notion did from the militaristic Prussian one in the nineteenth century. It is a fact, however, that many African writers see a fundamental tension between the Western, or liberal, or romantic concept of individualism, and that which they label as the corresponding 'African' idea.

---

[1] Lovedale Press, South Africa, 1930, 1957. See my article entitled 'Peter Abrahams' in *Critique*, vol. xi, no. 3 December 1968, and also the appendix to this volume, in which some relevant passages appear side by side.

Dabula is an army captain, the young disciple of Gubuza, the commander of the king's armies, and Mkomozi, his wise (one might almost say Westernized) witch-doctor. His development to consciousness, or full individuality, is the linking device Abrahams uses to give continuity to the Matabele section of the book, and to relate it to contemporary developments in the Boer camp. In the latter respect his counterpart is Anna, who develops from a position of relatively uncomplicated and unconscious domesticity (which is not much more than hinted at) through the total trauma of the Trek and all the specific conflicts it causes to a point of self-knowledge—and knowledge of others—which in its unbearable clarity contributes to her death.

Dabula, too, is sort of innocent when we meet him, engaged in soldiery at which he is expert, bothered by only one conflict: whether to remain faithful to his only wife (having been encouraged by the example of Gubuza, his mentor, to take only one, contrary to tribal custom), or to experiment with other women. Abrahams uses a type of stream-of-consciousness technique to render the young man's conflicts, such as they are. (A similar technique, as has been seen, was used for Anna.) As he sits listening to Gubuza and Mkomozi talk, he indulges in this reverie:

> No one had told him that he had to sit here and listen. Gubuza had not said 'Dabula, stay with us and listen to our wisdom.' Yet here he was ... So he sat here listening to the old men and hearing the laughter and gaiety of the young men over there. Why? ...
> ... His mind said: You are here because you are a creature of Gubuza. You do the bidding of Gubuza without his telling you. Rebellion stirred in him. Why should he do the bidding of Gubuza any more than any other warriors? And something else inside him said: You are disloyal in your thoughts. Gubuza is a father to you. He is your father. He took you in and brought you up as a child. All you have is due to Gubuza. He wondered if it would have been the same if Gubuza had really been his father, if Gubuza had been the man who had slept with his mother and brought him forth. How does one know these

things? It's like having only one wife. You do not know how it feels to have many wives. This, too, was the doing of Gubuza. He had only one wife because it was the wish of Gubuza. Maybe it was right, as Gubuza said. But how could he know, having only one wife? And why were the others against him?[1]

The conflict grows more acute, as Gubuza and Mkomozi discuss rumours of the advent of strange men with white skins from across the sea. Dabula gets up.

'I am going for a walk.' He had not meant to say it. He had meant just to get up and walk away but it had tumbled out. Always it was like this. Always, he made explanations when really he did not want to. He walked away from the fire hurriedly.

No! Not another woman.

Ntombi's breasts are sharp and pointed. You feel them when you lean against them. They press up against you and make your flesh tingle ... Are there really other lands across the waters? ... Would another woman be as warm as Ntombi? Would it feel the same ... And they have hair that is straight, the old man said. And if I had my own father, would I feel the same about him ... Remember the time Ntombi laughed and cried at the same time? She nearly tore a hole in my back then. What a night that was! Cannot forget that night ever ... How do they live across the waters? How do they make huts with corners? Strange, that. Huts with corners. Funny. Makes you want to laugh ...[2]

It may be hypersensitive to suggest the presence of a tone that is basically patronizing in this treatment of Dabula's thought processes, and a technical correspondence exists between them and the treatment of some of Anna's internal monologues. But the level of operation in Dabula's case is so superficial and unconvincing that one cannot avoid the conclusion that Abrahams was unable to make up his mind about the imaginative treatment of his Matabele characters. He cannot make them fully archaic because they would be unrecognizable in

---

[1] *Wild Conquest*, pp. 171−2.   [2] *Ibid.*, p. 175.

terms of their Boer counterparts: but to treat them as ordinary human beings appears to be beyond the scope of his imagination. So they are, most uneasily, somewhere in between.

Dabula's conflict is clearly intended to stand for something larger and more all-embracing. The area of doubt—polygamy —represents the pull between old and new. Dabula is in between: he succumbs to the force of tradition (and sexual desire) and sleeps with a young virgin betrothed to the chief of a subject tribe. But afterwards he forbids her to tell anyone, thus possibly condemning her to be cast out when her husband discovers that she is no longer intact. For this he is plagued (most unconvincingly) by guilt, until, after several unrelated adventures, he tells his wife of the escapade: they part on equivocal terms when he is summoned by the king to search for *his* favourite wife who has gone missing. He finds her among the Basuto, where he is subjected to a crash course in modernization by Moshesh, their wise and westernized king who has concluded a treaty with the British. Moshesh sends a message to Gubuza through Dabula not on any account to fight against the advancing Boers, but to negotiate while Moshesh arranges with the English to support them against the Boers. But Dabula returns too late with his message because Gubuza, in the grip of events, has decided to fight, and even the advice of his respected friend Moshesh will not deter him. His grounds for this decision are interesting:

'For myself I have often thought and wondered about the coming of these people. Ever since my friend, Moshesh, spoke of them many years ago. Sometimes I thought their coming might bring new wisdom that would put an end to our fighting. I thought they might come in peace. If they had come thus, I, Gubuza, would have gone to them and said: "Wise men from the seas! I come to sit at your feet that I might learn your wisdom." I would have gone to them and said that! But they came in the name of war! They come speaking the old language of blood and wrath, the old language of war. Oh, where are my hopes! They come with new ways and weapons but no new wisdom! Then, let them come! Even if I die, I would meet them and test their weapons with my blood. Even thus would I avenge the vain hopes that were born in me when I heard of their coming. . . .

'. . . I am for war! Let us crush these strangers or die, for after their coming the land will be desolate and there will be much weeping in the hearts of the mothers of our children. They bring no new wisdom! They bring new means of death!'[1]

This indicates the closeness of Gubuza to Paul Van As, the young man whom he fatally wounds and momentarily communicates with before they die side by side. Both he and Van As, crudely speaking, are for peace and progress: yet when the chips are down, each chooses to fight in spite of his doubts and principles: each makes the same initial sacrifice, and each loses all. Gubuza's diction in the speech in which he announces his choice would be justifiable on the ground that the occasion is in a sense ceremonial, or official, if it were not that the same pseudo-archaisms and stilted tone characterize him—and all the other Matabele characters— at all times, which makes for monotony.

In any event, Gubuza recognizes Dabula's growth to maturity and he leaves him with a charge, before he goes to his death:

'If the battle is against us, mount your pony and hurry to Inzwinyani. Tell Mzilikazi to go north, to lead the people there, till they cross the great Limpopo. Tell him to set up a new kingdom there. Tell him I say he must try to rule with the wisdom we found together . . . That is all for Mzilikazi. For you there is much.

'You will be the new general of the king's armies. Train your men well in the arts of battle, but shun war. But the most important duty I demand of you concerns young Lobengula. He will be king soon for his father is old and will soon die. You must be the guardian of the young boy. Teach him the wisdom you have learned from me. Teach him also the wisdom of Moshesh. Teach him not to fight white men but to intrigue

---

[1] *Ibid.*, pp. 321–2.

with them and make treaties with them. Teach him to be cunning in the ways of peace. . .'[1]

Gubuza's message, which is fundamentally the same as Paul Van As's, thus has a better chance of surviving and being transmitted than Paul's does, since the latter dies in mid-sentence— 'Teach . . . our . . . child.'[2]

Similarly, Dabula survives *his* Boer counterpart, Anna, who, like him, has had to acquire consciousness and understanding through experience, often unpleasant, in the course of the book.

Thus the fundamental distinction that Abrahams seems to make between the Boers and the Matabele (who are, of course, historical analogues for white and black South Africans at the present time) is made in terms of humanist values: he sees their extinction among the Boers, whereas among the Matabele he sees hope for their transmission and survival. This impression is strengthened by the fact that while Anna's marriage, which has been destroyed through her husband's susceptibility to the prevalent atmosphere of hate, ends in her accusation of him with her dying breath, Dabula's, despite his episode of unfaithfulness, moves to reconciliation and renewed strength. On his return from Thaba Bosigo his wife tells him she has been to the village of the girl he slept with and found that instead of being an outcast she is the chief's first wife:

'The first wife. . .' he relaxed.
    'Yes. She is very happy and the chief loves her much.'
    'Ntombi. . .'
    The laughter touched her mouth. The tightness left him completely. He reached forward.
    'The child,' she warned.
    She put the child on the blanket. He pulled her to him and held her tight. They stayed like that for a long time. . .
    'You have changed,' she said.
    How did she know? Mkomozi knew it too. But what was this change in him? If only he could understand that. . .

---

[1] *Ibid.*, pp. 342–3.   [2] *Ibid.*, p. 346.

90

'I must go,' he said.

'I will wait for you to come back.'

'I will come back.'[1]

The impression of the Matabele as having a great humanist future, even when compared with the Boers, is weakened to the point of extinction, however, by its arbitrariness in the face of the sustained picture of the Matabele produced by the book as a whole. In fact, one gets only broad outlines: a bloodthirsty, irresponsible people, given to singing, dancing and drink, ruled over by an ageing king and squabbling, intriguing generals, unaware of anything beyond their own immediate reality, at the mercy of witchdoctors with political ambitions and hypnotic powers, and in every way as bad as, if and when not worse than, the Boers. This background is boldly drawn, and it is not enough for Gubuza and Mkomozi and the king to deplore the bloodlust of the people after a night's successful witch-hunting, nor do the senile and solitary mutterings of Mkomozi suffice to correct this general impression or to bring it alive by filling in the vital details. Mkomozi is much addicted in times of crisis to climbing the western hills above the royal city and communing child-like with an imaginary companion.

> ... Tonight, his thoughts were addressed to those strange white creatures from across the sea. Would they know of Inzwinyani? Would they know of its meaning? Of the treachery and the feasting and the fears and dreams? If one of them was here with him now, would he know? ... Oh, brother! Have you not seen Inzwinyani on a feast night? Really? Oh, my brother! Where are you from, man? ... What is your name? ... What your tribe? ... Listen!
>
> Night is over Inzwinyani. The moon is big. Like a bright yellow ball that is white at the same time. If you are a dreamer you reach up and touch it, brother. And the stars, they are like a brood of over-bright children round mother moon. There is no sky, no sky at all. There is only the moon and stars and space. Nothing else up there.

---

[1] *Ibid.*, p. 332.

And the moon is on the earth, too, brother. A young moon that lights up the grass on the earth. As I say, if you are a dreamer you can touch it, brother . . . Moon and stars and grass on the earth. See the brightness on the river, brother. It is the moon and the stars again. They are in the sky and they are in the water. Even the water dances. It knows of feast night in Inzwinyani.[1]

And so on. Scarcely the kind of solid, detailed insight needed to give the white stranger any idea whatsoever about Matabele society. As for the novel-reader—well, he need not feel compelled to endure this sentimental mystification. Abrahams is at his worst with Mkomozi, which points to his central problem in this novel (which is, incidentally, manifested in several other ways): how to convey realistically the idea that the Matabele are the repositories of positive values. Fundamentally, this is the problem of how to present the Matabele convincingly in any light—which, on a more general level, is the widely encountered difficulty in African literature of producing satisfactory African characters. Abrahams never solves the problem, but has recourse to hoary and outworn novelists' tricks. Thus my criticism of Mkomozi is different from Mphahlele's, who complains that he lacks conviction when he takes the cosmic view of life but is credible when he 'contemplates things within the limits of his community's experience'.[2] What if those very things, the author's portrayal of Mkomozi's community's experience, are basically unconvincing? Abrahams has failed on two connected levels: to find an adequate idiom for the expression of tribal African life, and to establish a cosmic frame of reference from within a tribal idiom. Mkomozi's pathetic failure as a character comes directly from Abraham's inability to overcome this central problem.

In terms of the overall structure of the novel, it is interesting to note the large number of images of disintegration the author

---

[1] *Ibid.*, pp. 217–18.
[2] E. Mphahlele, *African Image*, p. 179.

uses. This is particularly remarkable in terms of marriage relationships. The first of these to come to an end is that of Paul, the son of Johannes the head slave, and his wife Lena. Paul is shot dead on the Jansen farm by Koos Jansen. Then the marriage of Kasper and Anna goes through its lengthy and painful disintegration. Paul and Elsie Van As are separated by Paul's death. Dabula and Ntombi's marriage undergoes the crisis that has been described: Mzilikazi, the Matabele king, has one wife put to death for inducing another to flee from him: the marriage of Gubuza and Nanda ends with Gubuza's death in battle. The one thing that all these marriages have in common is that they have all been at one time well-founded and happy; where this happiness has been destroyed, it has been by an extraordinary event.

This series of disintegrations in human relations establishes clearly the pessimistic tone which informs the book. It is thus a departure for Abrahams from the stylized Marxist optimism maintained before its appearance. His characteristic pattern of strong female and weak male figures is still present. The elements of sentimentality joined with violence persist, and characters and events continue to suffer from an overload of symbolic intent. It is, perhaps, the best organized of his novels before *A Wreath for Udomo*; but the only ingredients that are radically different from what went before are the uncertain and pessimistic liberal humanism that takes over from the facile Marxism of the earlier works, and the more detached authorial point of view.

One of the major structural weaknesses which requires examination, growing as it does out of one of the book's most successful sections, and being connected too with the adoption of this new ethical standpoint, is the treatment of the former slaves. The first forty-five pages of the book are concerned with the relationship between the Boers in the Cape and their Coloured slaves. The events described are dramatic and momentous. Abrahams' characterization of the members of the slave community is much more successful (particularly in the case of Johannes, their leader) than anything he manages with the Matabele. Johannes as a source of wisdom, particularly when he attempts to define freedom in a way that his fellow-slaves will understand, is far more convincing than the childish Mkomozi or the theatrically unassuming Moshesh. A little slave-girl asks him the meaning of the word:

'It is many things to many people,' he said slowly, but even as he said it he knew it meant nothing real to them. Suddenly, a vision of the house in the valley shot into his mind. Yes, that would do it. That was the way he could tell them . . .

'Come with me' he said. 'Come with me and I will show you what I mean.'

He took the little girl's hand and led the way out of the shack . . . The others fell in behind . . . And the procession that numbered fifteen of the twenty-five slaves owned by Kasper Jansen and his family, moved slowly up the side of the mountain till they stood where they could see the whole valley, and, far in its recesses, the sprawling white farmstead.

The morning sun had climbed to a point almost directly overhead and beat down hotly on them and on the valley and on everything in it. It threw a hard and brilliant light over the land and some shaded their eyes as they looked. The blue of the sky was bright.

'Look at it,' old Johannes said. 'Do not look at the house only. Look at the house and the earth and the trees and the beasts. All that you see belongs to the Jansens, to Kasper Jansen and his family. Yet, we, all of us, we built the house and tilled the earth and got rid of the weeds and planted the food and looked after the cattle.

'Think, my people. Would it be so wrong for that to belong to us? We made it.

'Before I was caught and made a slave, what I made was mine. If I built a house, it was mine; if I planted a tree, it was mine. And no one could come and take what I had made from me.

'Often have I heard Kasper Jansen and his friends talk about freedom. But for them it is something else. They have the valley and the house and the earth and what grows in it. Perhaps if we had it too, freedom might mean something else. I don't know.'

He turned his eyes to the little girl and put his hand lightly on her head.

'The child says "what is freedom, papa?" I say: when that valley belongs to us, and that house belongs to us, and when the things we build and the food we grow is ours, and when we and our children can eat and sleep in that house and there is no Baas Koos and no Baas Kasper to take what is ours, I say that is freedom. That is the kind of freedom I want for my children and my wife and myself and for all of you . . . [He refers to a runaway slave who tries to incite them to violence.] It is the kind of freedom Jan cannot understand. Jan's freedom says burn the house and the grain. Mine says let us live in the house and eat the grain.'[1]

Ironically, Jan's idea of freedom seems to have something in common with the hatred felt by the Jansens for their slaves, because Kasper Jansen fires the farmhouse before he leaves, to prevent his former bondsmen from living in it.

One might have been led to believe that the emphasis laid on this issue of freedom and slavery suggests that it will persist as a theme through the rest of the book. The delicacy and sureness of the writing in this passage would also appear to indicate a degree of centrality for it. But the slaves themselves, after putting out the fire in the farmhouse, are left hanging on a peculiarly optimistic note:

The fire was gradually being brought under control.

A wordless prayer, a prayer of feeling and desire and hope, rose up deep within the old man and flowed over the children of the ex-slaves and over the ex-slaves and over the burning house and over the valley and the mountains till it reached up to the skies.

Wordlessly it said: 'That ye might have life, and that ye might have it more abundantly.'

When the fire was under control and the people turned to him, [Johannes] said: 'My people, now we can begin. The valley is ours . . .'[2]

---

[1] *Wild Conquest*, pp. 19–21.   [2] *Ibid.*, p. 57.

Whether the irony is intentional or not is impossible to determine. The slaves, except in a couple of references to Johannes as the symbol in Kasper Jansen's mind of all black men whom he hates, disappear. Their fate becomes unimportant. One might have liked to have known something of it. Do they found a sort of socialist utopian community, an extended family kibbutz, or do they, too, disintegrate despite the enlightened efforts of Johannes? How long is it before the white man catches up with them again, as he does the Matabele in Rhodesia? There is no good reason why the group of people should be abandoned suddenly, apparently, like the Matabele at the end of the book and much more convincingly so, somehow, a repository for hope in a better future, but without any indication of what that future would be: particularly as there are glaring opportunities, even needs, for the thematic integration of this first part of the novel with the rest of it. On top of all this, the first part of the first section contains much of the best writing in the book. The violent disjunction which follows the end of it is altogether too arbitrary to be borne.

Perhaps the key to Abrahams' intentions lies in the central paragraph in Johannes' definition of freedom, which runs:

> 'Often have I heard Kasper Jansen and his friends talk about freedom. But for them it is something else. They have the valley and the house and the earth and what goes with it. Perhaps if we had it too, freedom might mean something else. I don't know.'

He is suggesting that the entire Trek is based on an illusion, on a false notion of freedom. There is evidence for this in the sick power of the Boer rhetoric, when the predikant curses the 'kaffirs' with the word of God[1] or when Hendrik Potgieter, the Trek leader, addresses the trekkers:

> '... Behind us we left the fruitful land of our birth: we left it that we might be free, that we might speak our own language and worship God in our own way.

---

[1] *Ibid.*, p. 30.

'Ahead lay many trials and dangers, but also the land. We will take that land and build our homes and farms there. We will build a new State and a new people there ... dedicated to freedom ...'[1]

This is persuasive, and the whole issue of slavery seems to be forgotten; but perhaps Abrahams intends it to be *the* underlying issue (for which in the bulk of the book there is no significant evidence): if it is, then the book in a sense hinges on Johannes' definition of freedom. But if this is indeed what Abrahams intended, then he failed precisely because he has not integrated part one of book one structurally or thematically with the rest of the novel; the disjunction between it and the rest is too violent.

The novel also marks the beginning of Abrahams' alienation from those forms of African nationalism or Pan-Africanism orientated towards the traditional past in Africa. His rejection of tribal life is not as fully explicit as it becomes in *A Wreath for Udomo*: the conscious commitment to Western liberal humanism is also rather exclusive—a not unknown phenomenon among other Western authors who lose faith in their youthful Marxism. In Abrahams the rejection of the tribal group leads to (or is accompanied by) a total involvement with the typical liberal humanist preoccupations with the fate of the individual and his need for and prospects of personal fulfilment, in relation to himself rather than society. This has its clear beginnings in *Udomo*, but its foundation is in the rejection of the group, of man in the mass, implicit in *Wild Conquest*: and it develops in Abrahams' later work into the peculiarly aristocratic position (which includes a strong feeling of mixed fear and contempt for ordinary people) of his last two novels, *A Night of Their Own* and *This Island Now*.

---

[1] *Ibid.*, p. 144.

5

Travel and Autobiography

In 1952 Abrahams, whose reputation as a writer had for the time being been established by the favourable reception of *Wild Conquest*, was commissioned by the London *Observer* to visit South Africa and publish a series of articles reflecting his impressions of the racial situation. The two books which resulted from this visit demonstrated that he was uniquely well qualified for his task. The first, *Return to Goli*, a work of reportage, appeared in 1953, and was succeeded in the following year by the dramatized autobiography *Tell Freedom.*

These books, especially the former, represent problems for the critic in that they cannot be ignored in any approach, however puristically literary, to Abrahams' work, because they bulk large in his canon and deal with events that shaped decisively his course as a novelist. At the beginning of *Return to Goli* he hints at the existence of powerful internal pressures which made his return to his birthplace a matter of personal necessity. The book opens with an impressive account of his own position on racial issues, and some of the events and factors that had determined this. The major part of this account took the form of a broadcast talk on the BBC early in 1952, and Abrahams quotes it, presumably in full. It constitutes the point of departure for his investigations and judgments while in South Africa; but its significance goes further than that, as far as his literary work is concerned.

He concludes his talk by suggesting, arbitrarily, that there are 'three levels of living'.

First, there is the basic struggle: the struggle for life, which is the struggle for bread, home and security. This is the instinctive struggle of all animals. On the second level, this basic struggle is charged with social content and consciousness. The protection of the individual is the security of the group. The greatest loyalty is to the group, the nation, the race. The moral values of the group are, implicitly, superior to those of all other groups. This group exclusiveness is usually hidden, but is seen at its most blatant in times of strife and war. It makes for the super-patriot, for the fanatic nationalist. But on the last level the mind takes hold of the instinct. The will casts out fear. Shelley says:

> Sceptreless, free, uncircumscribed, but man
> Equal, unclassed, tribeless, and nationless,
> Exempt from awe, worship, degree, the king
> Over himself; just, gentle, wise ...

Such is the freedom of the last level: the level of the whole man, freed, ultimately, from his fear. It makes such beautiful sense of E. M. Forster's hope that he would have the guts to choose his friend should the choice arise between friend and country.[1]

Having established the pedigree of his liberalism centrally in the English bourgeois romantic tradition—and none the worse for that—he ties up his anecdotes about disaffected black friends into a prophetic warning, against some of the fallacies that disillusionment with liberalism lead to:

> On that level no Negro would be either proud or ashamed of being a Negro. And in his fight to be free he would not counter bigotry with more bigotry, prejudice with more prejudice. He would know that to do so would be to lose for his fight its contact with history, with the 2,000-year-old journey of man from darkness to the stars. And if he loses that contact, the battle will be lost, though won.
>
> The Negro can say: 'This is not of my doing. The world of white men drives me to this extreme position.' He would be justified. And, with justification on his side, he would be lost.

---

[1] *Return to Goli* (Faber and Faber, London, 1953) p. 26.

But, fighting on the level of the last freedom, we fight for light against darkness; for all humanity, not black, or white, or pink humanity only. And fighting thus we will transform ourselves from half-men into men. The world is a dark place now. But fighting thus, with our eyes on the last level, the morning star will lead us. It is there for the seeing. Raise your head! Look up, my love, look up![1]

Earlier in the talk he expresses his worry that black reaction to white racism in its various forms is leading black intellectuals into a racialist prison of their own making:

I think three conclusions can be drawn. First, large numbers of Negroes tend to reach out for prejudice, even where it does not exist. Second, many Negroes tend to be double-faced and dishonest in their relations with non-Negroes. Their white friends, even their girl friends, are dismissed, when not present, as 'like all whites'. Third, many Negroes are building up a colour bar of their own. They would counter South Africa's 'Reserved for Europeans Only,' with their own 'Reserved for Negroes Only'. They would counter bigotry with bigotry, hate with hate, darkness with yet more darkness.

To me, these three points add up to an act of racial discrimination against self. More than that, they go counter to the very real and very profoundly human base of genuine Negro aspirations. Still more, they go counter to the timeless, raceless, and nationless aspirations, that lie dormant in most men everywhere, for a full life on the last level of living. And that is a crime against humanity.[2]

That his insight in such matters is not only delicate on a personal level but possesses a certain historic power is borne out by the subsequent emergence of the 'ideology' of black power—even though this negates the optimistic tone of his conclusion. In this context it is interesting to note, parenthetically, how frequently Abrahams asserts his feeling of identification and harmony with English society.

---

[1] *Ibid.*, pp. 26–7. [2] *Ibid.*, pp. 25–6.

It will be clear that Abrahams' conscious adoption of a fairly undiluted form of the ideology of English liberalism is related to his personal experience of a very great contrast. As he himself pointed out:

> But all this had been worked out a long way from the seat of the problem. It was comparatively easy to work out a tolerant and humanist view of life in England. England had been kind to me. It had given me the chance to build a decent dignified life for myself. In it I had learnt to laugh and play, and found my love. It had given me access to forms of beauty. Its climate of mental freedom had allowed me to pursue my thoughts as far as they would go, and without fear. And I had made true friendships there.
>
> It was because I had myself become unembittered that I had been able to work out this view of life. But was it a true view? Was it really mine? Could it stand the strains and stresses of life in South Africa, or, indeed, in any of the other plural societies of East and Central Africa?
>
> There was no way of knowing except by going there. My faith had to be tested on the battlefield of race hatred. Only thus could I be certain.[1]

It is centrally important to the understanding of his fiction to appreciate its development as a long process of testing, or a series of tests of, this ideology so foreign to his own early experience. For that is the contrast mentioned earlier: basically it is that between those who could afford to be humane, tolerant, liberal, whose background and education had given them the comfort, leisure and security to imbibe humanistic values, and those whose formative experiences were harsh and deprived, consisting of a continuous awareness of the need to struggle, and a persistent knowledge that the results of the struggle were continuously unsatisfying.

Tell Freedom may be said to stand as a necessary (and meticulous) examination of this contrast, preliminary to the major

---

[1] *Ibid.*, pp. 27–8.

phase of testing the values he has chosen. In these two books, then, the objective facts are established: in *Return to Goli* on a broadly-based social, economic and political level and in *Tell Freedom* on the level of the individual. These facts constitute the essential materials for Abrahams' literary trial of liberal values, which stretches throughout his work. These two books enhance his earlier achievement by placing it precisely in its personal historical context, revealing (unconsciously, no doubt) the nature of the particular disadvantages he has had to work under: and they prefigure the themes and topics of his later work, as well as illuminating in an unusual and interesting manner their major stylistic faults and merits.

The fascinating connection between his most characteristic stylistic lapses and certain kinds of content in the novels is paralleled in these two works. The standard example is that of dialogue. In general Abrahams handles this badly, especially in his later novels, in which ideas predominate so decisively over action. Yet in *Return to Goli*, writing with himself as the first person participant in conversations involving the same ideas and problems as those he deals with fictively in, say, *A Night of Their Own* or *This Island Now*, one finds a freshness, a quality of liveliness, an ingredient of humour, indeed of humanity, which is almost always absent from parallel situations in the novels. One need only contrast these two passages, the first from *Return to Goli* and the second from *A Night of Their Own*, to perceive the extent of the difference between Abrahams' fictive mode and his style of reportage:

> After the mountains we relaxed. The passengers moved about and began to fraternize. The old gentleman in front of me, an ex-mayor of one of the big cities of South Africa, got into conversation with me. It went something like this:
> 'Going to West Africa?'
> 'No. South.'
> 'To the Union?'
> 'Yes.'
> 'Why?'

'For a visit and to do some writing.'

'Ah, you're a journalist. Only South Africa?'

'Kenya too. And perhaps some of the other territories if there's time.'

'You'll find it very interesting.'

He called another old gentleman and said:

'He's a journalist. He's going to South Africa and then your part.'

'Ah-ha,' the second gentleman said. 'What paper?'

'The *Observer*,' I said.

'That's a good paper,' the first said.

'Trouble is you're always criticizing us,' the second said. 'You make out there's nothing good about the white people in Africa.'

'I don't think you can charge the *Observer* with that.'

'Then it's the others,' he said. 'I say most of the English papers are writing a lot of nonsense about us.'

'If you go and see and report honestly,' the first said, 'you'll find it's not like the English papers make out. They all talk as if there's blood and violence and hate. It's not like that at all. You'll find us happy and peaceful and not like the papers make out.'

'Tell me,' said the second, 'what exactly are you going to look for? Most of you journalists go out to find fault.'

'I'm going to see what race-relations are like.'

'The colour bar?'

'Yes. That and other things.'

'You don't understand about this,' said the first.

'None of you people in England do.'

'What don't we understand?'

'About this colour bar. Now, there's no bar for you because you're civilized. In England you can do as you please and go where you please. Is that right?'

'Yet.'

'Well now, our people are not the same as you people are. They are still uncivilized and backward.'

'All of them?'

'Yes.'

'Aren't there any educated ones?'

'Yes, but it's not the same. You're different. Anyone can

see you're a civilized man, and being civilized is not just book learning. All you people are different. Your people are more developed than ours are.'

'Anyway, there's no colour bar in our part,' said the second.

I turned to the ex-mayor.

'But I come from South Africa. I was born there, in Johannesburg.'

He looked startled, then refused to believe me.

'No. You come from West Africa.'

'I was born in the Union. It's true, you know.'

'I don't believe it.'

The second said:

'You don't speak or behave like anyone from South Africa—or East Africa for that matter.'

'Like a West African?' I asked.

'Yes,' he said. 'Like an educated one who's been in England for a long time.'

'I have been in England for a long time. But I still come from South Africa.'[1]

A shadow flitted across the woman's face, a minor emotional convulsion; then the automatic, polite smile that he remembered from other awkward times showed on her face.

'You've lost weight, Karl—but it suits you.'

'What do I say?'

'Two years is a long time. I'm not surprised you find it awkward.'

'Please, Mildred.'

'All right! What am I supposed to do? Fall on your neck because you've condescended to come back? Or is it that you've become infected with what you profess to detest?'

She turned her back on him and found a chair. Briefly, he was consciously aware once more of the strong scent of roses. Every corner of the room had a large vase of roses.

'I wrote you, Mildred. I explained.'

'And explanations cancel all hurt! Explanations make the blind see and the halt walk and the crooked straight!... Please don't tempt me into saying what I don't want to and don't

---

[1] *Ibid.*, pp. 33–5.

mean. The thing is: I took you at your word. We had agreed that we would be honest and say when either of us couldn't take it any more. You were staying away; you had chosen to. That was the fact. The explanations were unimportant—ways of justifying or excusing a decision. The fact was that you were not coming back and I adjusted myself to this fact. And now . . . '

He cut into her words, with a quiet casual insistence familiar to her from other times: 'I don't know where I'm going any more. . . .' . . .

. . . He said: 'D'you understand what I'm saying, Mildred?'
'I'm trying to.'
'If you do, you'll understand why I wrote and why I'm here.'
'If not?'
He shrugged and walked away from where she sat. 'Then I might as well give in.'
'Give in?'
'To the hate-mongers and the fear-mongers.'
The woman thought: There was a time when I leaned on him and he gave me strength and comfort and confidence; but that was oh so long ago. And now?
'Have you eaten, Karl?'
'I don't want anything.'
She got up and went out of the room. When she returned, she poured two drinks for them.
He came to her and said: 'Please, may I touch you?'[1]

It is difficult to account for such a marked difference except by concluding that Abrahams is not a 'natural' writer of fiction, and that when he uses the tools of his chosen trade they turn out to be blunt and clumsy rather than sharp and incisive. The parallel, however, goes further that this: in certain situations we find similarities rather than differences:

If you are a stranger, man, walk with me and I will guide you. A man needs a guide here, for this place can be strange to a stranger. When I first came here there was no one to guide me. I was beaten and stabbed and robbed of all my money and my clothes. You must watch out, for this is a city of gangsters.

---

[1] *A Night of Their Own* (Faber and Faber, London, 1965), pp. 168–7.

Hush, man, don't be foolish! What do you think you can do with your stick and your strength? These gangsters do not attack you singly or with sticks. First thing you will know of it is when you lie bleeding. Walk carefully, brother, and forget your strength. Black men? Of course they are Black men like us. But they are not really like us, you know. They are children of this place. They were born here and they do not know the farms and the country. The past? How can they know of the past? I tell you, man, they are children of the city. Most of them have never heard of Chaka or Dingaan or Moshesh or Mzilikazi.[1]

'And this other thing of which there are so many rumours, tell me of that?'

Dabula thought: How deep his voice is. But I've known it all my life.

'The white men?' Mkomozi asked.

Dabula let his thoughts be and listened.

'Yes,' Gubuza said.

'There are such men,' Mkomozi said.

'Many?'

'I don't know. But you must know of them.'

'I know of wars other tribes have fought with them, but that is all.'

'I have seen them,' Mkomozi said.

'Are they really white?' Dabula asked.

'Yes. They are white, my son.'

'Where did you see them?' Gubuza asked.

'Many years ago I went to the coast. To a place they call the Cape. I saw them there.'

'Tell us of them,' Gubuza urged.

A flame shot up tall and bright, and Dabula saw the old man leaning forward. But for his face, it could have been a young child leaning forward.

'When you first see them they are strange. Not like people at all. Their hair is straight and they have a lot of it. Their skins turn red in the sun and it is as if the blood would fall out of their skins. They wear garments in the shape of the

---

[1] *Return to Goli*, pp. 91–2.

body of person. . . .'

Dabula tried to see one of these people but his mind could not build up the picture.

'. . . Their huts have corners to them and they are big, bigger than any of the royal huts I have seen. I saw some where one hut is on top of the other.'

'Strange,' Dabula murmured.

'And their wisdom?' Gubuza asked.

'Of that I cannot speak. I was not there long. And they spoke a language that I could not understand.'

'But you know all languages,' Gubuza said.

'Not theirs. It is like no language you have ever heard.'

'Has it no relation to the languages of the north, of our past of which you so often speak?'

'None at all.'

'Have you been in their huts?' Dabula asked.

'No.'

'Where are they from?' Gubuza asked.

'It is said they are from across the waters.'

'Are there lands across the waters?' There was doubt in Dabula's voice.

'For strange people to come here, there must be. They must come from some land for people can live only on land. The people across the great desert of the north are fair but not like these. So there must be other lands.'

Other lands! Other people! And white people with a language that even the wisdom of Mkomozi cannot understand! Strange indeed. Dabula tried to think of it, to grasp the meaning of these things.[1]

The contortions which Abrahams' dialogue undergoes immediately he deals with African characters have already been remarked upon and they will, no doubt, attract our attention again. The appearance of this irritating phenomenon in works generally free from most of his other less fluent stylistic mannerisms is an indication of the limited range of experience within which Abrahams is able to operate with confidence. This is not to say that the narrative tech-

---

[1] *Wild Conquest*, pp. 172–3.

nique he employs in *Return to Goli* to render African life on the mines or in the city is an unsuccessful one. Far from it; and it is handled with a competence, dignity and sincerity far exceeding that of Truman Capote and his successors in the briefly fashionable school of the 'documentary novel' which was questionably based on a similar methodology to that deployed by Abrahams in *Return to Goli* and *Tell Freedom*. The fact is that Abrahams feels desperately remote from an area of experience he knows to be vitally important for him to incorporate within the scope of his fiction. As a result he has had to overlay his unfamiliarity with a heavy-handed helping of technique. That this area of failure springs from a genuine and consciously recognized imaginative difficulty is borne out by its appearance in a genre in which most of his technical weaknesses are virtually absent. The consequences for his success as a novelist are plain and far-reaching. It is interesting to compare the technique and general effects of the beginning of chapter four of *Return to Goli* with the extracts taken from the late Henry Nxumalo's famous exposé of farm labour conditions in Bethal, Eastern Transvaal, originally published in *Drum*, which Abrahams quotes later in the same chapter.[1] Here is first person narration of experience by Africans which is crisp, unaffected, unspoiled by technique, and immediate, and the contrast with Abrahams' own attempts is telling. It is clearly not just an example of the well-known contemporary novelistic difficulty (much canvassed in theory) of the rendering of 'ordinary people'. Abrahams appears to be faced with a genuine creative block, which is certainly not based on race or colour, as his efforts in *A Wreath for Udomo* and *This Island Now* show. In situations where the colour factor is not as important as the author himself thinks, the difficulty turns out to be an inability to extend the creative imagination to encompass the experience of groups which lie outside the main stream of the Western cultural experience. What is fascinating about this is the lateness of Abrahams'

---

[1] *Return to Goli*, pp. 123–8 and 133–5.

personal arrival in this stream. That is what *Tell Freedom* is about.

As the *New Statesman* reviewer pointed out, the novelistic element in *Tell Freedom* is quite organic to the work. It is in no sense 'pure' autobiography, but a highly dramatized, one is even tempted to say experimental, version. It proceeds out of two levels of need, both hinted at in the opening chapter of *Return to Goli* and both embedded in the text of the work itself. One is the autobiographical urge to explain and justify which is felt by nearly all writers—the basic human need to identify oneself, to be understood for what one is and has become: the other, the need to give information about objective conditions, which is not surprisingly rather emphatic in this book, in view of the conditions themselves and the author's relationship with them.

These two needs develop into the opposite poles of the inner tension which determines the structure of the book. Each of these is an aspect of Abrahams' personal experience: the shared reality of millions of poor and oppressed people, those who do not escape, but live out their lives within the system Abrahams describes—this develops out of the descriptive level; and the differences, the distinctions, the crucial turning points which led to the complete differentiation of fates between Abrahams and all those who did not get away—this is the product of the need for self-definition.

Thus Abrahams' development is presented as a process of differentiation, a gradual loss of innocence and growth of awareness of the nature of the particular historical and social forces which govern his situation as a human being.

The first half of the book is dominated by the pole of similarity. The emphasis is on the identity of objective experience between the young boy who is the focus of attention, and the remaining members of his group. Although he is presented as sharply distinct from other characters, a classic novelistic 'centre of consciousness', he does not at this stage provide any interpretation of his experiences. He is involved in a number of incidents of increased intensity, such as the following:

The long summer days hung over Vrededorp. And to ease the length of each day, I searched for new forms of adventure. One day, some boys down Twenty-second Street asked me to go coal-hunting with them. There were four of us. We each had a little sack.

We climbed over the high, pronged fencing that cut off the railway lines from the streets of Vrededorp.

'Watch out for police,' a boy called.

We ran between the lines, picking up pieces of coal. Goods trains trundled along; expresses flashed by. We shouted and waved at them. When they had gone we carried on with our search. The boldest of our numbers, a pot-bellied, bare-chested black boy saw a large pile of coal near a stationary wagon.

'Here!'

We followed him. We were shoving coal into our sacks when one boy suddenly shouted:

'Trap! Run!'

I turned. Two men, one black, one white, were nearly on us. I dodged an outstretched arm and shot away, leaving my sack. Heavy feet thundered after me. From somewhere behind I heard a boy scream in pain. The thundering feet were very close. If they caught me I would go to a reformatory and get lashes. I ran as hard as I could. Oh, God! The fence is so far away. Run, Lee, run. They'll lash the skin off your back at the reformatory. I'll never steal coal again, *baas*. Never again. Those boys made me do it. I streaked over the lines, heart pounding. I sensed a hand reaching out for me. I dodged. The man behind me over-balanced and went down heavily. I was safe. The fence was near. I would have time to climb it and fling myself to the ground on the safe side. I reached it and shot up to the top. Then the seat of my pants got caught on one of the prongs. I worked furiously to get it loose. I looked back and saw the man drawing near. It was the black one. He raised his stick and flung it. It caught me on the side of the face. The weight of my body, falling, ripped my pants off the prong. Dazed, I fell on the Vrededorp side of the fence.

When I became aware of the world, I was surrounded by a crowd of angry, shouting women. One of them had the stick which had felled me. She brandished it at the man on the other side of the fence.

'He's my prisoner,' the man said. 'And that is my stick. I'm coming over for them.'

'Come!' the woman shouted. 'Come, you dog of the white man! We will show you where your manhood was lost!'

'A child,' another said bitterly. 'See the blood on his face. A child!'

'They were stealing,' the man said.

'So you, a grown man, must use a stick of battle on an un-armed child. Come over and we will kill you! I will kill you with my own hands!'

'It is my work,' the man said. 'A man must work to live.'

'So you, a black man, must go on even after the white man has given up!'

'A black man!'

'But it is my work,' the man protested.

'Our work is to protect our children. Stone the dog! He has sold his manhood to the whites!'

The man turned and ran. A rain of stones followed him. They flung stones long after he had gone.

The woman who had picked up the stick examined my face. There was a cut on the side of my right eye.[1]

In this extract the victim could be any non-white slum child in South Africa, and thus the episode itself possesses a general application. The boy does not realize that he has been nipped by the pincers of colour: it is his rescuers, the women who save him, who place the incident in its political and moral context.

The structure of such episodes remains the same throughout the first part of the book. In these incidents the centre of consciousness, the young Peter Abrahams, is not distinguishable from any other Coloured slum boy of his age. The operative technical element is a separation amounting to a contrast between innocence and experience. The young perceiver merely undergoes whatever is happening to him, without being aware

---

[1] *Tell Freedom*, pp. 68–70.

of any implications further than the immediate. Other, older, more experienced characters involved in the same incident, invoke these implications (which are those specifically related to the racial set-up in South Africa) for the reader: but even this spelling out is without meaning to the young sufferer, and he merely records it without adding any gloss of his own.

Episodes of this kind are the pillars which hold up the structure of the first section of the book, and they are linked by descriptive material of day-to-day experience which successfully conveys the hardships of poverty without necessarily suggesting a determining context of race:

> There was a sharp bite to the morning air I sucked in; it stung my nose so that tears came to my eyes; it went down my throat like an icy draught; my nose ran. I tried breathing through my mouth but this was worse. The cold went through my shirt and shorts; my skin went pimply and chilled; my fingers went numb and began to ache; my feet felt like frozen lumps that did not belong to me, yet jarred and hurt each time I put them down. I began to feel sick and desperate.
>
> 'Jesus God in heaven!' Andries cried suddenly.
>
> I looked at him. His eyes were rimmed in red. Tears ran down his cheeks. His face was drawn and purple, a sick look on it.
>
> 'Faster,' I said.
>
> 'Think it'll help?'
>
> I nodded. We went faster. We passed two children, sobbing and moaning as they ran. We were all in the same desperate situation. We were creatures haunted and hounded by the cold. It was a cruel enemy who gave no quarter. And our means of fighting it were pitifully inadequate. In all the mornings and evenings of the winter months, young and old, big and small, were helpless victims of the bitter cold. Only towards noon and the early afternoon, when the sun sat high in the sky, was there a brief respite. For us, the children, the cold, especially the morning cold, assumed an awful and malevolent personality. We talked of 'It'. 'It' was a half-human monster with evil thoughts, evil intentions, bent on destroying us. 'It' was happiest when we were most miserable. Andries had

told me how 'It' had, last winter, caught and killed a boy.

Hunger was an enemy too, but one with whom we could come to terms, who had many virtues and values. Hunger gave our *pap, moeroga*, and crackling, a feast-like quality. We could, when it was not with us, think and talk kindly about it. Its memory could even give moments of laughter. But the cold of winter was with us all the time. 'It' never really eased up. There were only more bearable degrees of 'It' at high noon and on mild days. 'It' was the real enemy. And on this Wednesday morning, as we ran across the veld, winter was more bitterly, bitingly, freezingly, real than ever.

The sun climbed. The frozen earth thawed, leaving the short grass looking wet and weary. Painfully, our feet and legs came alive. The aching numbness slowly left our fingers. We ran more slowly in the more bearable cold.[1]

The success of writing like this comes out of direct experience, vividly and imaginatively recreated after a long interval. Abrahams' failure to integrate this material into his straightforward fiction is a puzzle; it is as if the consciousness of writing fiction inhibits his performance, not that he lacks descriptive ability. Indeed, certain qualities which inform the writing in *Tell Freedom*—qualities such as humour and liveliness—are precisely those most lacking in his works of fiction.

This structural principle of peak and trough is not an end in itself. Gradually the youthful perceiver begins to react, at first through his feelings and then intellectually, when he is trapped in the eye of one of these storms. The turning point comes when he goes with his sister and his brother's fiancée to visit his older brother Harry, who is serving fourteen days at Diepkloof Reformatory (of which Alan Paton was later headmaster) for a petty offence:

The afternoon sun slanted westward, but only slightly. A lone eagle circled overhead. Once, it spread its great wings and swooped down low. No doubt to see what manner of men these striped beings were. Then, with movements of great power

---

[1] *Ibid.*, pp. 32–3.

and grace, it climbed. It made an almost straight line up. I watched it grow smaller, hazy, and then merge into the blue sky that had suddenly grown infinitely far removed from the world of men. I longed, suddenly, to be like that eagle, able to fly right out of the range of this place, so that I would not have to watch my brother breaking rock under the hot sun.[1]

The symbolic contrast between the eagle's power and the impotence of the prisoner and his relatives, and the storm in heaven and apparent calm on earth indicate a development in the way in which the young boy perceives experience. This is the first time an event evokes from him a clearly-defined imaginative response, in which a connection is made between different levels of activity—though it is significant that the young Abrahams as centre of consciousness still makes no mention of colour in his reaction to the episode. This is for the last time left to his adult companions. The closing sentence of the episode is staggering in its definitiveness, its sense of the inevitable: '"A gang of prisoners will always remind me of my brother," Maggie said.

This closes a phase of the young hero's development, and the pace of the writing is immediately quickened as Abrahams moves straight into two more episodes of heightened intensity. In the first, three white youths waylay the young Abrahams on an autumn day as he returns home from work. One of them demands that he fight him, and beats him, scientifically and without mercy. Half-conscious, he is rescued by an African, who asks him: '"Why did they beat you, son?" "They say because I'm black," I said tiredly.'[2]

This, it should be noticed, is the young Abrahams' first response purely in terms of colour, and it is a masterpiece of restraint. The word 'tiredly' suggests the buckling of a particular kind of resistance, the natural resistance of innocence, of the child's purity of perception, against the ugliness of the

---

[1] *Ibid.*, pp. 135–6.
[2] *Ibid.*, p. 142.

reality of evil. The cumulative battering of the facts concerning colour has forced a way into the consciousness of the young boy. The resistance has ended; the damage is likely to be permanent.

The next episode follows immediately and occupies two lines: 'Another time, a white man on a cycle cleared his throat and spat as he flashed by. The muck struck me in the eye . . .'[1]

Thus the first phase of development reaches a climax with the opening of a necessary wound in the young hero's sensibility. The next shows, essentially, the various attempts he makes at first to assuage the pain, and later to heal the wound.

The beginning of this phase is clearly marked. The ten- or eleven-year-old Abrahams is working as a solderer's boy in a smithy: in his spare time he cleans the owner's car, and is given sandwiches in return. Once, on going into the office to claim his reward, the 'short-sighted Jewish girl' typist challenges him:

'Lee.'
I stopped and turned to her.
'That is your name, isn't it?'
'Yes, missus.'
'Miss, not missus. You only say missus to a married woman.'
Her smile encouraged me.
'We say it to all white women.'
'Then you are wrong. Say miss.'
'Yes, miss.'
'That's better . . . Tell me, how old are you?'
'Going on for eleven, miss.'
'Why don't you go to school?'
'I don't know, miss.'
'Don't you want to?'
'I don't know, miss.'
'Can you read or write?'
'No, miss.'

---

[1] *Ibid.*, p. 142.

'Stop saying miss now.'

'Yes, miss.'

She laughed.

'Sit down. Eat your sandwiches if you like.'

I sat on the edge of the chair near the door.

'So you can't read?'

'No, miss.'

'Wouldn't you like to?'

'I don't know, miss.'

'Want to find out?'

'Yes, miss.'

She turned the pages of the book in front of her. She looked at me, then began to read from *Lamb's Tales from Shakespeare*.

The story of Othello jumped at me and invaded my heart and mind as the young woman read. I was transported to the land where the brave Moor lived and loved and destroyed his love.

The young woman finished.

'Like it?'

'Oh yes!'

'Good. This book is full of stories like that. If you go to school you'll be able to read them for yourself.'

'But can I find a book like that?'

'Yes. There are many books.'

'The same one with the same story?'

'There are thousands.'

'Exactly like it?'

'Exactly.'

'Then I'm going to school!'

'When?'

'Monday.'

'I've started something!' She laughed. 'But why didn't you go before?'

'Nobody told me.'

'You must have seen other children go to school.'

'Nobody told me about the stories.'

'Oh yes, the stories.'

'When I can read and write I'll make stories like that!'

She smiled, leaned back suddenly and reached for her pen.

She opened the book.

'Your surname?'

'Abrahams, miss. Peter is my real name, Peter Abrahams.'

She wrote in the book.

'Here, I've put your name in it. It's for you.'

I looked at her writing.

'That my name?'

'Yes. I've written "this is the property of Peter Abrahams".'

'But which is my name?'

'Those two words.' She pointed. 'Well, take it!'

I took the book. I held it gingerly. I moved to the door, backwards. She shook her head and laughed. The laughter ended abruptly.

'Oh God,' she said and shook her head again.

'Thank you, miss. Thank you!'

Her eyes looked strangely bright behind the thick glasses.

'Go away!' she said. 'Go away . . . and good luck . . .'

I hesitated awkwardly at the door. Was she crying? and why?

Yes, thank you, miss. Thank you![1]

(One may as well remark in passing that nowhere in his novels does Abrahams manage dialogue as skilfully or as naturally as in *Tell Freedom*. In this instance the casual rhythm of everyday speech comprehends the nuances of this particular encounter between white and Coloured, at the same time effectively concealing the magnitude of its significance, which is rendered by the adult Abrahams' appearance at the end of the extract, echoing the innocent words of the child's gratitude but endowing them with an understanding of what was begun on that occasion.)

The tension between innocence and experience is still present, but from this point the gap begins to narrow, and the polarity becomes a dynamic relationship between two aspects of the same person, the writer and his younger self—a characteristic autobiographical technique.

---

[1] *Ibid.*, pp. 149–51

Also from this point one is aware of a progressive increase in emphasis on the elements of distinction between the life experiences of Peter Abrahams and the 'average Coloured boy' of his age, who hovers as a sort of ghostly objective correlative in the background, as a further series of turning points is presented, each confirming and extending the process of separation. Abrahams' description of the effect of schooling shows how his inner conflict reflects this bifurcation:

> I attended school regularly for three years. I leaned to read and write. Lamb's *Tales from Shakespeare* was my favourite reading matter. I stole, by finding, Palgrave's *Golden Treasury*. These two books, and the Everyman edition of John Keats, were my proudest and dearest possessions, my greatest wealth. They fed the familiar craving hunger that awaits the sensitive young and poor when the moment of awareness comes.
>
> > *Bards of Passion and of Mirth*
> > *Ye have left your souls on earth!*
> > *Have ye souls in heaven too,*
> > *Double-lived in regions new?*
>
> With Shakespeare and poetry, a new world was born. New dreams, new desires, a new self-consciousness, was born. I lived in two worlds, the world of Vrededorp and the world of these books. And, somehow, both were equally real. Each was a potent force in my life, compelling. My heart and mind were in turmoil. Only the victory of one or the other could bring me peace.[1]

The hero is at this stage immediately aware of the conflict: no adult sensibility is required to interpret it. About this time he goes for long nocturnal walks to the white areas of Johannesburg, where he sees splendour, warmth and luxury, and he finds the vision attractive, but of course it is forbidden him by the ubiquitous slogan of white South Africa's moral superiority: 'Reserved for Europeans Only!' The mature Abrahams comments:

---

[1] *Ibid.*, p. 161.

> The familiar mood that awaits the sensitive young who are poor
> and dispossessed is a mood of sharp and painful inferiority, of
> violently angry tensions, of desperate and overwhelming long-
> ings. On these nightly walks, that mood took possession of me.
> My three books fed it.[1]

His schooling is inevitably interrupted by the Depression,
and the result for him is to close somewhat the widening gap
between himself and his background. Certainly on the most
concrete level the direct effects of the Depression on his life
must have resembled closely those on many other gifted and
sensitive Coloured children.

Abrahams becomes a market-boy, a ragged and dirty newspaper vendor, then a cruelly-exploited cleaner in a hotel. He
returns to carrying the bags of white women shoppers at the
Johannesburg market, an activity that is illegal and undertaken
in the face of police vigilance, when one day at a coffee stall a
well-dressed young black man sees that Abrahams is reading his
newspaper over his shoulder. What happens is enormously
revealing, as well as (by chance) possessing the most crucial
importance for the development of the phenomenon which we
now call, however unsatisfactorily, 'African literature.'

> 'Can you read?'
>   I nodded.
>   'Really?'
>   'Yes.'
>   He looked me over. A half-smile touched his lips and creased
> his handsome face.
>   'All right. Here, read this to me.'
>   I took the paper and read aloud.
>   'By God, you can, too!'
>   'I told you. I went to school.'
>   'Then what are you doing here?'
>   'Working.'
>   'At the market?'
>   'Yes.'
>   'Why?'

---

[1] *Ibid.*, pp. 164–5.

'I want money to learn some more.'

'And you're one of those who stop white women and ask to carry their bags . . .'

'Yes.'

'Couldn't you find a better job?'

'No.'

'Did you try?'

'I tried hard.'

'And that is why you carry white women's bags?'

'Yes.'

'Incredible!' He shook his head and burst out laughing. 'Like another coffee and fatcake?'

While I ate, he kept looking at me. He seemed unable to control his laughter. He was laughing at me. It hurt. I could endure the laughter and mockery of whites. But this, from a black man, hurt. I put down the mug and walked away. He came bounding after me, and grabbed my arm.

'You are wrong, my friend, you are wrong. I wasn't laughing at you. I was laughing at myself. I'm sorry. Come back and I'll explain. Honestly.'

He led me back to the stand.

'Have another coffee and cake with me. . . . I really was laughing at myself. At myself and all the others like me. You see, we despise you. Among ourselves, in our clubs and homes, we say it is you and those like you who make things difficult for us. We see you barefooted, dirty, running about the streets and markets. It makes us ashamed. We say the whites see you and think all blacks are like you. We say they never meet us, the educated, the teachers. So, to them, all blacks are the same. And we blame you for it. We do not try to find out about you, we just blame you. And how wrong we can be! It was that which made me laugh. You showed me how foolish and prejudiced our own people can be. That was all. I felt ashamed of myself and my laughter was against me and hid my shame. All right?'

'All right.'

'What do you want to learn?'

'To write stories.'

'I cannot help you there. But maybe I can help with a job. Do you know the Bantu Men's Social Centre?'

'No. But I can find it.'

'Good. Go there. Ask for Mr Peter Dabula. Describe me to him and tell him I said he might have a job for you.'[1]

Two things emerge from this almost miraculous coincidence which possess considerable significance. One is the fortuitous nature of the encounter whose results were to be so far-reaching both for Abrahams as an individual and, arguably, for the future of a particular style of literature on the continent of his birth. The world he describes is certainly not one in which the rewards of virtue are automatic. The times are crushingly hard, and the lucky emergence of one fifteen-year-old from privation and inevitable eventual submersion in the common fate of his people can only be seen against a background composed of those thousands of equally well-endowed young men and women who did not escape but remained, despite whatever efforts they could exert, within the oppressive framework of their Coloured destinies. Which leads to the second point of significance. Apart from the chillingly arbitrary workings of luck (which approach alarmingly close to the level of a theme in the book) what emerges from the incident is, in a way, Abrahams' essential *passivity*. He is on the receiving end: his experience has taught him the pointlessness of aiming too high. After being forced to leave school he tries but fails to find work as a messenger boy: so he accepts the killing inevitability of market carrying and newspaper selling. His fortuitous meeting with his black benefactor only emphasizes how far from unique his situation had been up to that moment, and how easily the gifted, the talented, the sensitive fall back from their precarious individuality to the general level of common deprivation in situations of social stress.

And the essential hopelessness of the spiritual situation of the non-white groups in Southern Africa, quite apart from the economic hardships of the Depression, is revealed by the young man's initial response to Peter. They are all trapped within the values

---

[1] *Ibid.*, pp. 187–8.

of the community which rejects their every humblest aspiration, their merest desire for basic humanity to receive minimal recognition. The well-dressed young black teacher is a victim of the values of the white middle class whose aspirations are forever denied to him: he even accepts a crucial aspect of white prejudice against his own group: but he has never had the opportunity of learning or adopting any other system. He rejects Peter at first because the latter's appearance fails to measure up to the standards of 'white' respectability. One perceives how the trap operates, how all the non-whites, black and Coloured, educated or illiterate, well-dressed or in rags, are caught in it, how it constitutes for them the very process of living, and how it distorts their perceptions, warps their values, and prevents the emergence of the essential solidarity required to bring about a change.

It has been pointed out that *Tell Freedom* and *Return to Goli* contain many of the sounding boards whose themes echo throughout Abrahams' fiction. The entrapment of the oppressed within the oppressors' value system is found operating powerfully in his earlier novels, up to *Wild Conquest* ; though the author's attitude to the values themselves is ambivalent, moving from an envious and confused rejection, expressed in the fate of Lisa in *Mine Boy*, to a reasonably uncritical acceptance (Mabi and Lois in *A Wreath for Udomo*) and finally to disillusion, which emerges strongly in *This Island Now*.

Also present in the encounter between Peter and the young black teacher is a very subtle and successful instance of the informational level of the book in operation. Abrahams is reduced to the level of a character in a book, who listens: the information extracted by the reader (and this is carefully controlled by Abrahams the *author*) has been obtained from what Abrahams the *character* has been listening to—but it becomes available to the reader without the ostensible assistance of either of Abrahams' personae. He doesn't shove the conclusions down our throats; no adult character is present at the encounter, judging the black teacher's words; nor does the young Peter put any gloss or interpretation on them. But certain essential items of knowledge come the reader's way, needed for a complete understanding of the position of the black group in South Africa, and therefore of what makes Peter, the central character, tick.

This account of Abrahams' technical mode explains the general success of the function of the book as a provider of objective information about a particular situation. The information is very seldom free-floating, as it were: in almost every case it is organically connected with the hero's situation, which is general enough, potentially symbolic enough, to prevent the informational level of the enterprise from foundering on the rocks of egocentricity. From this point on the individual, distinctive Peter Abrahams emerges very clearly. He is always seen against a background, but now the relationship between him and it becomes contrastive, not assimilative. Yet tensions persist, and the path for the new Abrahams tends in the direction of increased complexity and difficulty, even if it is one more familiar to his readers, as the stock escape from poverty and deprivation that has constituted a standard theme in Western literature—and life—since the novels of Dickens.

The starting point is carefully noted in the book. With dramatic appropriateness, it occurs on his first day at the Bantu Men's Social Centre:

I went down to the library and my newly discovered *New Negroes*.

We shall not always plant while others reap
The golden increment of bursting fruit,
Not always countenance, abject and mute,
That lesser men should hold their brothers cheap;
Not everlastingly while others sleep
Shall we beguile their limbs with mellow flute,
Not always bend to some more subtle brute;
We were not made eternally to weep.

A man called Countee Cullen said that to me. And this man loved John Keats in a way I understood.

A man called Langston Hughes said:
I'm looking for a house

In the world
Where the white shadows
Will not fall.

Then he checked me with:

There is no such house,
Dark brother,
No such house
At all.

There were many others. Sterling Brown wrote with the authority of a man who had had a long talk with history. Claude McKay stirred me to aggressive pride:

Oh, Kinsmen! We must meet the common foe;
Though far outnumbered let us still be brave,
And for their thousand blows deal one death-blow!
What though before us lies the open grave?
Like men we'll face the murderous, cowardly pack,
Pressed to the wall, dying, but fighting back!

I could go out and spit in a white man's face! . . . Fortunately, the mood passed long before I met a white man.

Georgia Douglas Johnson stirred me to pride in the darkness of my mother and sister; and Jean Toomer

Carolling softly souls of slavery,
What they were, and what they are to me,
Carolling softly souls of slavery,

stirred me to the verge of tears.

In the months that followed, I spent nearly all my spare time in the library of the Bantu Men's Social Centre. I read every one of the books on the shelf marked: American Negro literature. I became a nationalist, a colour nationalist through the writings of men and women who lived a world away from me. To them I owe a great debt for crystallizing my vague yearnings to write and for showing me the long dream was attainable.

My mother came from Vrededorp that night and we had a little family party. I told them about my job and about my discovery of American Negro literature. I tried to tell them what it meant to me. But they were not really interested. America and Harlem were at the other end of the world. And in Coloured terminology Negroes were black people whom both whites and Coloureds called Natives in their polite moments. I gave up my attempts, sat back, and listened. They talked happily about the little rounds of their days. I realized, quite suddenly, that I was rapidly moving out of this Coloured world of mine, out of the reach of even my dear mother and sister. I saw them with the objective eyes of a stranger. My mother touched my arm.

'You're growing up fast, Lee . . .'

I looked into her eyes. Her lips curved in understanding. She had caught my thought. *She* was still with me.[1]

This historic first encounter with American Negro literature is seen, significantly enough, in terms of a *self*-realization, not through the interpretation of an outsider or an adult sensibility. And the encounter is historic for reasons which have been mentioned: if Abrahams' ambition to become a writer was fired in the furnace of this new discovery (and there is no reason to doubt his assertion that this was the case) then the decisive influence of the very fact that he had written and published books, upon individuals as diverse but as important for the development of African literature as Ekwensi, Ngugi, p'Bitek, dates back to this precise moment.

The remainder of the book really belongs to the category of social or political history. It presents an interesting but in most ways conventional picture of the young Coloured intellectual, having achieved his entry by a mixture of luck and determination into the rarified realm of the best in non-white education, and having undergone the prescribed spell at the Anglican boarding-school in the country, and then St Peter's Rosettenville (which bred many of South Africa's non-white political and intellectual leaders until the government closed it down), finding his way and his identity in the world of left-wing politics and journalism, where the fact of colour is as far as possible relegated to its appropriate level of significance. Abrahams loses his virginity to a white girl, and is snubbed in the street by another, out of necessity, as she is walking with her racist employer (the book is

---

[1] *Ibid.*, pp. 196–8.

partly dedicated to her). Feeling stifled on the level of personal relationships he goes to Cape Town, becomes involved with the wealthy Trotskyist Gool family, participates again in left-wing politics, and once again feels defeated on the individual level. Since Marxism fails to resolve his individual isolation, he rejects it and undertakes a cross-country odyssey to Durban, walking, hitch-hiking and living off the land (one feels that a fine literary opportunity lies unexploited here) and spends a year with poor young Indian political activists and intellectuals in Durban before managing to be taken on as a trimmer on a ship bound for England, shortly after the outbreak of war.

There are two high points in this final section of the book. The first is the brilliantly sensitive and perceptive evocation of the fate of non-white intellectuals in South Africa. It is suggested to the young Abrahams with devastating tact and helplessness by Fezile Teka, once a prominent journalist and writer, who was already experiencing the fundamentally destructive frustration so inevitable in the situation:

I visited the office of *The Bantu World* next morning. Mr Teka received me warmly. He was a young man with shrewd, kindly eyes and a very dry manner. He sent for tea and we talked. He asked about my college. We talked about books and poetry.

'We talk about you sometimes,' Teka said, 'We worry about your future. You know the Dhlomo brothers write in the vernacular. There are one or two others. The only place they can publish is the Lovedale Press. And they must be careful what they write. Well, we wonder about you. You write in English and already you are touching things that should not be mentioned. See what I mean?'

'Yes, I see.'

'Good. We say among ourselves: "He can become a teacher but even then he will have to be careful what he writes or else he will have to put it away." And someone else says: "If only he were in another land." And another says: "There is no future for him." See, your poems have reached us. And we think and talk about you; and we wonder and hope.' He leaned back and raised his eyes to the ceiling. 'We hope, my friend, we all hope. We know the road is hard but still we hope. Perhaps it is unfair, but we hope.'

A boy brought in the tea. Teka's mood changed. He talked about his home and childhood with amusing dryness. I gave him a batch of new poems. He made a little pile of three half-crowns and pushed them to me.

'It is not much but a man wants to help . . .'[1]

This frustration leads inevitably to despair and moral disaster, as the lives of so many non-white writers, whether they chose home or exile (and what sort of choice was it?) show. The names of Can Themba and Henry Nxumalo spring to mind— the one drinking himself to death in lonely exile in Basutoland without confirming the brilliant promise of his short stories and sketches, the other knifed to death in mysterious but not uncommon circumstances one weekend in the township. But these fates merely represent the end of a long and brutal period of existential despair, of the extinction of the creative torch. It was not possible then, and it is not now, to be a teacher or a writer or an intellectual or a journalist if you are a non-white South African—the relevant qualifying colour has to be inserted, and it constitutes a killing frustration. Abrahams' acceptance of this realization was a factor in confirming his early need for escape. There can have been few more sensitive or percipient observers of the results of the system for the individual than Abrahams at that time. In the light of his almost instinctive attraction to the values of liberal individualism, his refusal to be deceived by the illusory satisfactions of political involvement, and his decision to seek his personal salvation by leaving rather than salving his conscience by becoming involved in what he saw to be a dead end on a deeper level than that of political success, was no desertion or surrender but an act of courage and consistency.

The concluding chapters of the book also contain what is perhaps Abrahams' finest achievement as an exponent of imaginative realism. It is a short sketch of his involvement as a schoolteacher in a bitterly poor community on the desolate Cape

---

[1] *Ibid.*, pp. 232–3.

Flats—also the setting for Alex la Guma's novel, *And a Three-fold Cord*. He beautifully realizes the character of Roderiques, the failed priest, who involves him in the venture, and his descriptive passages on the physical condition and plight of the inhabitants of the community are full of power. The atmosphere of deprivation evoked, however briefly, is reminiscent of Solzhenitsyn's *One Day in the Life of Ivan Denisovitch*. The writing is economical, the eye for detail sharp, and the mode is above all realistic, and free from the sentimentality that plagues his fiction. The whole sketch is too long to quote and there is no point in mutilating it since it is very neatly organized. Its presence in *Tell Freedom*, rather than one of the novels, eloquently expresses the paradoxical status Abrahams occupies as a writer of fiction.

There is one other point of interest in the last section of the book, which clarifies part of the background to Abrahams' eventual adoption of the values of European liberalism. It is also significant in the light of Ulli Beier's well-known criticism that he ignores what is valid and creative in African culture both past and present. He describes his friendship, while a boarder at Grace Dieu in the Northern Transvaal, with an African fellow-pupil named Jonathan, and uses the latter's first visit to the city to make clear his own position in regard to the 'technological gap'; what he felt European civilization had to offer to Africa, and where it failed. The speaker is Jonathan:

> A boy is satisfied with his village, and the life of his village, because he knows no other. That is his life. That is the life of his ancestors before him. And, for him, it is a good life. He herds his cattle and observes the rules and laws of the tribe. He is content.
>
> And then the white man comes into his contentment. The white man shows him new things and new ways. And he is no longer content with the old ways. The white man says the key to this world is to become a Christian and to have knowledge and education. The boy looks at the things of this new world. He finds them good. The toilet where the chain is pulled and

the waste matter is flushed away, is cleaner, healthier, and more desirable than the hole in the ground or the foul-smelling can that is cleared two or three times a week; clean running water from taps means healthier lives and the end of the many water diseases of the well, the river, or the unclean spring; the journey by train is faster and more comfortable than the long trek on foot or by ox-wagon; roomy houses that let in air and light so that a man wakes fresh in the morning are superior to the dark, airless huts of old; electric lights instead of grease lamps and darkness; the superior medicine of the white man; oh, a whole world of new things makes the new world more desirable than the old.

And so he becomes a Christian and he goes to school. Knowledge brings new desires, new beliefs: the god of love in place of the pagan gods of war of old; the new view of the stranger, the foreigner, as a brother to be welcomed rather than an enemy to be destroyed or feared; long dreams of a new life; new ways of thinking and responding open to him. The vision of the humble Christ, the father of all men, of all races and colours, supplants the little gods of old. And so the boy turns his back on the old world of his ancestors, opens his arms wide, and reaches hungrily for the new, superior ways that offer a whole new world. And so, a new man, he goes to the city to see and get to know. All his future, now, will be linked with the city. Even if he is to spend the rest of his life in the country, he must go to the city because it is the symbol of this new world . . . .

Jonathan's quiet voice was silent for a while. He turned his dark face so that I saw only a stern profile.

'It is difficult,' he said.

'Yes,' I said.

'I went to the city,' he said. 'And I learned these things are not for me.'

'I told you,' I said.

'I did not believe. You know how the boys from the cities lie.'

'Yes.'

'They should have told me. I believed it was for me too. It was wrong for them not to tell us . . . .'

'Would it have changed anything?'

'I don't know. But it is better to know. . . . Did a white

person ever spit in your face?"

He turned his face to me again. I looked into his eyes.

'Yes.'

'In mine too.'[1]

This is a remarkably condensed passage assessing Abrahams' disagreement with those who advocate loosely-argued traditionalist theories of the virtues of tribal society. Abrahams begins in the best place, with the basic material conditions of life. His language is value-laden—nobody likes being told that someone else's ideas and practices are 'superior' to his own— and, in passing, on the basis of this passage one finds it almost incredible that it was ever found possible—or desirable—to argue for his inclusion within the negritude pantheon.

From the time Abrahams leaves St Peter's School, the direction of his strivings is clear. He wishes to establish himself as a man, as an individual with an integral identity and a prospect of fulfilment in freedom. It is a time-honoured Romantic position, which shows that flowers may grow in barren and stony places. It also gives shape to what has gone before, and as in all good autobiographies by young men, the end constitutes a new beginning. The summary of his experience and the aims which grow out of it rings the true note of European romanticism:

> For me, personally, life in South Africa had come to an end. I had been lucky in some of the whites I had met. Meeting them had made a straight 'all-blacks-are-good-all-whites-are-bad' attitude impossible. But I had reached a point where the gestures of even my friends among the whites were suspect, so I had to go or be for ever lost. I needed, not friends, not gestures, but my manhood. And the need was desperate.
>
> Perhaps life had a meaning that transcended race and colour. If it had, I could not find it in South Africa. Also, there was the

---

[1] *Ibid.*, pp. 235–6.

need to write, to tell freedom, and for this I needed to be personally free. . . .[1]

The stress is on personal relations, personal freedom, self-realization, fulfilment. It would seem that the South African experience produces some very good Europeans, after all.

---

[1] *Ibid.*, p. 311.

6

A Wreath for Udomo

A Wreath for Udomo (1956) marks the culmination of the second phase of Abrahams' creative development, and shows substantial progress towards artistic maturity. In a sense it is the result of crucial events in the author's life: a return for a visit to his family in South Africa, the self-examination produced by this, as well as the uneasy process of writing a work of autobiography. *Return to Goli* and *Tell Freedom* are Abrahams' best books: in them he achieves the fresh and honest realism he consistently falls short of in his novels. Writing them he was in a rich creative vein, something of which carries over to make *Udomo* his best achievement to date in the novel.

The second stage of Abrahams' development began with *Wild Conquest*, which was sharply distinguished from the preceding novels simply because it dealt with a major historical event, lengthily and in a fairly complex manner. Despite its other distinguishing features, which have already been discussed, it must be judged a failure, subject to many of the faults found in the early works. *Udomo* is similar in scope and deals with many of the same themes, but is much more advanced in technique, character presentation and the handling of moral issues.

A Wreath for Udomo is the story of a group of Africans involved in the struggle to free their continent from colonial rule. The book was highly topical when it was written, but few of its original readers who approached it sympathetically would have suspected it to be as full of prophetic insight as time has shown it to have been.

The novel is set in London and Panafrica (an imaginary country based on Abrahams' experience of Ghana), except for a brief and somewhat forced idyll on the southern coast of France. Panafrica borders on Pluralia, where the black majority is tyrannized by a white racist regime. Thus the major problems of Africa in the 'fifties are geographically juxtaposed for dramatic convenience.

The main thread of the story is concerned with the rise to power and downfall of Michael Udomo, who progresses from student agitator in London to first Prime Minister of independent Panafrica. Most of the action is conveyed through members of Udomo's circle: Lois, his intellectual Hampstead mistress, Mabi, the Panafrican artist, or Mhendi, the Pluralian revolutionary leader.

The characteristic themes of the second phase of Abrahams' writing are present in highly developed forms. They arise out of his political transition from naive historical materialist to committed Western Liberal, aware of individual shortcomings but retaining a superficial optimism in ultimate terms about the human condition in general. The cautious vagueness of the phrasing of the last sentence is deliberate: the optimism is really lip-service, and its shallowness is a sensitive indicator of the position Abrahams was to adopt in his next and most recent novels, the first of which appeared no fewer than eight years after *Udomo*. The clearest manifestation of Abrahams' liberalism is a deeply felt commitment to the idea of the human being as an individual.

The most obvious and perhaps startling result, in thematic terms, of Abrahams' conversion to liberalism, is the passionate identification with certain mythical beliefs of Western industrialized society, which are grouped around polarities such as 'past-future', 'primitive-civilized', 'corrupt-efficient', 'tribal-modern'. Indeed, the conflict between traditional and modern is one of the main themes of the book. The personal and political levels of action are inter-related by the operation of this theme in the lives of the major characters. Thus adherence to traditional social attitudes in politics is seen as a negation of in-

dividuality in personal life: towards the end of the book
Udomo feels that his erstwhile friend and cabinet colleague
Adebhoy, who betrays him and ultimately has him assassinated
for abandoning traditional ways, has 'gone back to the past of
blood ritual and ancestor worship. Really, Ade had always
been there; always a lying smile, like one of those old grimacing
masks from the past. Never a person because the person doesn't
matter; just a unit in a group. Someone he'd never known
because there had been no personality to know.'[1]

Mhendi, the Pluralian, in a long passage which is consciously
aimed at achieving a symbolic effect, sees the man rowing him
in a canoe across a great lake on his way to lead an uprising
against the white regime in his country as an analogue for all
the negative aspects of traditionalism, equated here (as elsewhere) with tribalism:

> In ... Out ... In ... Out ...
>
> Were these men human? Could ordinary mortals keep up
> this machine-like rhythm hour after hour?
>
> The sun climbed to a point overhead, stayed there, then
> moved westward. Mhendi began to feel light-hearted. Maria
> seemed in a daze where he could not reach her. His father had,
> as a young man, performed feats of endurance such as these
> canoeists now did. Men in the tribal state could still do this.
> The machine-age caught up with them. But what of the uglier
> side of tribalism? What of its greatest crime: the stifling and
> destroying of the human personality? ... The sun was far behind
> him now, on the western horizon. Was it the sun or was it really
> land, so close by? The chief canoeist was nodding at him,
> smiling. A human being again; not a unit in the tribal machine.
> Nodding and smiling? Then it was land.[2]

Traditionalism in its tribal aspect is also associated with
racism. Selina, the gaunt market-woman who is a sort of sinister
procuress to the revolution, makes her support of Udomo conditional on his not marrying a white woman, an undertaking

---

[1] *A Wreath for Udomo* (Faber and Faber, London, 1965), p. 302.
[2] *Ibid.*, pp. 216–17.

which for him involves much more of a personal betrayal than he is aware of. Selina and Adebhoy also institute the 'non-fraternization rule'; Abrahams makes the issue of 'Africanization' look unattractively doctrinaire and in effect racist, and an area of tension between Udomo and his traditionalist colleagues.

There are other attacks on traditionalism, most of them centring round tribal custom. The most interesting of these comes from Paul Mabi, the artist, who returns to Panafrica at Udomo's behest to become Minister of Education although he had sided with Udomo's betrayed mistress in England. Mabi, besides being Europeanized to his fingertips, represents a specially sensitive version of the liberal outlook; his artistic occupation is unmistakably symbolic. Mabi is especially furious because tribal custom prohibits him from seeing his mother on his return to his remote, mountainous and primitive home, until a lengthy collection of traditional ceremonies has been performed.[1] This is all rather unconvincing, since at no other point in the book has Mabi shown any eagerness to see his old mother, and presumably he could have done so at any time. He is in Panafrica, and indeed visiting his birthplace because Udomo has asked him to, not out of any evident compulsion to visit his mother, whom he appears to have ignored from London quite happily for years. Thus the *ground* of this attack on tribal tradition is rather suspect: but there is little question about the viciousness of the attack itself, or the fact that it directly reflects an authorial attitude.

The episode is rendered more interesting by the insight it gives us into Udomo's own attitude to the question, in action, so to speak. He is on an electoral tour and joins Mabi in the latter's home territory.[2] Despite the personal tension between the two men, Mabi is filled with admiration at the subtle way in which Udomo handles the tribal elders. Tom Lanwood, the elderly theoretician of the revolution, who has lived many years in England, has told Mabi how he cannot understand 'this

[1] *Ibid.*, pp. 230–8.   [2] *Ibid.*, pp. 240–4.

tribal business'; he is disillusioned and feels irrelevant to the local situation, which he has striven for years from exile to create. Udomo, on the other hand, seems very much at home:

> A young woman offered them fruit. Udomo took an orange and kissed the young woman's forehead. You do all the right things, Mabi thought. Then he saw the mocking, quizzical glint in Udomo's eyes.
>
> 'You'll be doing that too . . . Tom been talking?'
> 'Yes.'
> 'Thought he had. The tour upset him. He was distressed when they bathed my feet in blood at one place. Couldn't understand it. It made him sick.'
> 'What are we to do about tribalism?'
> 'Accept it. It's a fact. If I came out against it today I'd be out of office tomorrow. Accept it and attack it from the rear. That's the answer. That's why I'm pushing industrialization as hard as possible. That's why I need Mhendi's whites so desperately. Mhendi understands but neither Tom nor Ade do: Tom, because he's so bitterly horrified by it; Ade because he's such a staunch tribalist at heart . . . My greatest need is for trained men who are free of the tribal hold and yet understand it sufficiently to be diplomatic about it.'[1]

Thus Udomo is caught squarely in the middle of the conflict. His political development from naïve hero-worship conducted with great emotional intensity of Lanwood's Marxist brand of African revolutionary theory, to a sophisticated and pragmatic commitment, basically liberal in outlook, to the modernization and industrialization—in a word, the Westernization—of his country, is paralleled in his emotional growth. At the beginning of the book he is lonely and callow; his thought processes, boosted by volcanic surges of emotion, are adolescent, extreme, grand in scope, confused in detail. A typical reverie is found just before he commits himself to an affair with Lois:

> Pity Adebhoy was on night duty. But they'd all been wrong about Lanwood's woman. She'd been charming when he'd

---

[1] *Ibid.*, p. 242.

lunched there that Sunday. And very intelligent. Nice and warm down here. Will have to start thinking of finding a place for when Adebhoy leaves. That Colonial Office chap tried to be funny. Have to get the consent of the Panafrican authorities. Hell! They're the Panafrican authority. Shouting at him had made a difference though. They'd soon done something after that. Not much, but regular, and enough to tide him over. He'd got himself new shoes, shirts and socks, and that had taken all his first allowance. The consent of the Panafrican authorities! Brilliant idea this stencilled magazine. Fine article Lanwood had done: Mhendi too. Pity he drank so much. They'd all done fine articles really. Lovely idea those facts without comment. Let them condemn themselves out of their own mouths, these imperialistis. Good chap, Adebhoy. Hope Mabi's in.[1]

But as he matures his convictions change, his thinking becomes clear and organized, his goals explicit. Contrast the above passage with the preceding one, or with the climactic declaration of his position to Selina and Adebhoy just before they have him assassinated:

'. . . our country has three enemies. First, there is the white man. Then there is poverty, and then there is the past. Those are the three enemies.

'When I first came back I recognized only one of the three: the white man. But the moment I defeated him I saw the others, and they were greater and more dangerous than the white man. Beside these two the white man was easy, almost an ally. Well, I turned him into an ally against poverty. He works for us now, builds for us so that those who come after us will have bread and homes. There are schools and hospitals in the land. The young men and women are waking up. Why do you think I spent so much money sending them abroad? I'll tell you. Because I needed them as allies to fight our third enemy, the worst enemy we have: the past. I've paid lip-service to the ritual of ju-ju and blood ceremonies and worshipping at the shrines of our ancestors. Now I don't have to any more. There are enough liberated young people now for me to defy all that is ugly and evil

---

[1] *Ibid.*, pp. 49–50.

in our past. We can defeat it now. And you, Selina, and you, Ade, whom I once loved as a brother; you are the past. I'm going to defeat you! It is you who now stand in the way of Africa's greatness. Go on: fight me at the party conference and see who wins! You're too late, my friends. You're too late . . .'
He shrugged, smiled gently.[1]

Despite this growth he is defeated on both levels, at any rate in the short term. In a sense his conversion, or maturity, has come too late. Even though he boasts that the traditionalists were 'too late', that 'they'd given him too much time', it is time that defeats him in the end, on the less generous scale of the individual's life-span. His own growth has been to slow, and his commitment to the values of liberalism has come too late. He does *not* have time to redeem his betrayal of Lois; he is forced into a parallel betrayal of Mhendi to their common political enemy because of the weakness of a newly-established position. The second betrayal is in a sense worse because he is mature enough to understand its implications. But at the end of his life it is the first he comes back to and regrets most because it is on the level of personal relations, where there can be no consolatory successes.

The nature of the problem is delicately and effectively suggested when Udomo spends a brief and idyllic holiday with Lois in her cottage in an ancient French village:

On either side of the track the land was terraced. Vines grew on these terraces; miles and miles of vines going up and sideways.

They came to a dip in the steep slope of the land. A smaller track cut across the large track up to the mountains. They turned right along it.

'There it is,' Lois said.

The cottage stood in a large fenced-off piece of flat land. There were neglected fruit trees, an overgrown stretch of lawn at the side of the house, the remains of what had once been a child's swing; and in front of the house weeds had claimed what had once been a rock-garden.

---

[1] *Ibid.*, pp. 301–2.

Lois hurried on and opened the door. She stepped just inside the door, then turned and faced Udomo. Her face, suddenly, was that of a child.

'Welcome to my inheritance, Michael!'

He dropped his bag, stepped across the threshold, and folded her in his arms. She looked up after a while and her eyes were wet.

'You do do the right things, Michael.'

'It's important to you, this?'

'It's my dearest possession on earth.'

He ran his hand through her hair, grown long now.

'Say you love me,' she said.

'I love you,' he said.

'Oh, my dear . . .'[1]

Everything about the place suggests a long history of civilization of a particular kind; the terraces and vineyards convey a settled, cultivated pattern of living. The immediate surroundings of the cottage might connote the incipient decay of the system but it is still graceful and valid. Lois calls it her 'heritage', and the word reverberates through time and across the gulf between the two lovers of which the reader is suddenly acutely aware. For it is an unbridgeable gulf: however much he might want it to be, the cottage is *not* Udomo's heritage. And he *does* want it: as Lois says, he *does* do the right things. The surface appearances are in order, but time and place have conspired to make what Lois calls her 'dearest possession'—what the cottage symbolizes—the careful distillation of centuries of Western civilization into the precepts and values of modern liberal humanism—fundamentally inaccessible to Udomo and those who like him are destroyed by their desire for it.

Shortly after this he betrays Lois, suggesting the disastrous breadth of the gap.

The implications are far reaching and pessimistic. Udomo's slow growth into liberal maturity demonstrates that time is the individual African's greatest enemy. Udomo is not born into the

---

[1] *Ibid.*, p. 84.

heritage of Western liberal values. His induction into them is a trial, which not everyone is able to withstand. Their acquisition may be too superficial, and easily shed, as is the case with Adebhoy, or too thorough, which inhibits the will to act at the relevant time and place, causing moral squeamishness, as happens to Paul Mabi.

The prognostication is gloomy: the patient is doomed to die, if he is a liberal in contemporary Africa. Both Udomo and Mhendi are such people, and their fate is a result of their position in time, their personal situation in relation to historic processes. But it has another cause, which has its main fascination in relation to the development of Abrahams' thought: this is the fact that each of them engages in action. That the most distinctive thing about the modern liberal humanist is his inability or unwillingness to act decisively, to involve himself in a positive and forceful manner in almost any situation, has become something of a truism. The liberal's stress on the value of the individual has become mingled after the disillusion of two world wars with an appalled suspicion about the motives and consequences of almost any act. This is, of course, a pessimistic attitude, but it is one which is increasingly identified with Abrahams' heroes. Action leads to chaos—any action, any conscious involvement. In *A Wreath for Udomo*, Lois's involvement with Udomo ends in chaos and disillusion in her personal life and a withdrawal from her pattern of relationships into private inanition. Udomo acts methodically and purposefully to obtain an abortion for Jo, Lois's flatmate, whom he has made pregnant.

> The look of sympathy fell from Udomo's face as the door shut. He went back to his desk, closed his eyes. He thought of all the African medical students he knew in London. And as he thought, each one passed vividly before his mind's eye. He examined each with a cool critical detachment; he saw each face clearly, the kind of person each was, the degree of loyalty each would give, the reliability of each. At last he opened his eyes. He reached down under his desk and pulled out a card-index box. He took out a card from behind the letter T. He smiled

without humour. He slipped the card into his pocket, put the box back and rose. He went into the bedroom. He wrapped two woollen scarves round his neck and put on the dufflecoat. He heard Jo Furse in the kitchen. He went there.

'I've found our man. I'm going to see him now. I'll try and get him here tomorrow. You'd better get to bed before Lois comes. Say you're ill. And don't go to work tomorrow.'

'Will it be all right?'

'If you do as I tell you.'

He pulled the hood over his head and went out into the wafting snow.[1]

But the result of this action is unrelieved misery. Mhendi's devotion to political action (despite his many and characteristically liberal humanist doubts about its moral validity, which are enunciated with much greater clarity of thought than anything Udomo is capable of) leads to the killing of his first wife and his own shooting by the Pluralians, as well as the suicide of his widow. It is also interesting that the two characters who choose action, though their eventual goals are virtually identical, are set on an inevitable collision course. Thus action seems essentially negative and potentially destructive, and this is, as we have said, a viewpoint for which the contemporary liberal humanist is particularly noted. But Abrahams shows an interesting awareness of the dangers of passivity. Mabi, when he hears of Udomo's betrayal of Mhendi (from Udomo himself) reacts in a way which on the surface the liberal humanist must approve: he resigns from his ministerial position and returns to Hampstead to paint. But Udomo, who has sought his understanding and sympathy, eventually sneers at him:

'You want to be a patriot provided you can safeguard your precious soul. You know I had to [betray Mhendi]. Only, no dirtying of hands for you! Leave that to the foul Udomo. Mourning Mhendi indeed! He wouldn't want to be mourned by you. All right, go now, Mr Moral Mabi! I have to deal with realities, not your fancy ideas. You make me sick! Go . . .'[2]

---

[1] *Ibid.*, p. 109.   [2] *Ibid.*, p. 295.

Mabi later acknowledges the justice of Udomo's accusation that he has taken the easy way out: in a letter he writes to Lois at the end of the book, on hearing the news of Udomo's assassination, this crucial passage occurs:

But you and I, were we right with our private moralities? Can a man betray love and friendship, the gods we worship, and still be good? I think you'll still say no. Then how explain Udomo? I know the wrong he did you and Mhendi. But I also know the good he did Africa. Was he a good man? A great man? And is greatness beyond good and evil?[1]

The irony of this is that it is Mabi and Lois who have failed, ultimately, their own code. In Lois's complete withdrawal, in Mabi's refusal to respond to Udomo when he is 'talking, explaining, trying to make Mabi see his agony of spirit, his need for comfort',[2] they betray their very own humanist code based on the supremacy of the individual, the sacredness of personal relations, the deities of 'love and friendship'. Mabi's letter goes on: 'Oh how he [Udomo] grows on me as I think . . .'

This is entirely in keeping with two further characteristic failings of the liberal humanist, which Abrahams may not have been conscious of suggesting—an indication of the validity of his conversion: the 'secret admiration for men of action' identified by C. B. Cox[3] which is an attraction of opposites, and a tendency towards egotism, an overdeveloped and therefore paralysing and in a sense snobbish awareness of the uniqueness of the individual, leading to a refusal to 'dirty one's hands' on the grounds of imagined moral superiority. Thus Mabi is guilty of self-deceit, an error to which liberal humanists are particularly prone.

The weaknesses of the code (which is the book's standard moral reference) thus emerge, and assist in the general drift towards pessimism. The pessimism is perhaps a natural and even healthy reaction against the relatively firm framework of sentimentalized quasi-Marxist 'realism' that characterized the earlier

[1] *Ibid.*, p. 309.   [2] *Ibid.*, p. 292.
[3] C. B. Cox, *The Free Spirit*, (Oxford University Press, 1963), p. 1.

novels. It reflects the author's discovery of some moral relativism and the difficulty he experiences in coming to terms with it. At this stage in Abrahams' career this represents a positive development, a step towards maturity, as we have noted: what is not so reassuring is the future direction of this change, as we shall see.

Abrahams' view of the role of character has always been torn between the functional and the self-indulgent. The same could be said of Evelyn Waugh, so this is not altogether as damning as it sounds. Additionally, in *A Wreath for Udomo* (and to some extent in *Wild Conquest*) some of the ends which his characters serve are interesting and complex. Indeed, both books are, in a sense, structured around character, but *Udomo* shows a considerable development simply because it is about real, or at any rate believable, people.

In *Wild Conquest* the action is encapsulated, sealed off by the final sentences, contained within a historical period and therefore predetermined. In terms of character this isolation in time leads to allegory, flatness and stereotype. Each character constitutes a part of the total effect of a static picture, incomplete in himself and incapable of movement. This denies them the possibility of meaningful action; Abrahams' perspective is closed.

In *Udomo*, on the other hand, although he is again dealing with large-scale historico-political processes on a broad canvas, Abrahams employs a completely different attitude to time. Events take place on a developing, open-ended continuum, susceptible to influence from the vagaries of individuals as well as objective forces. Although a sense of the inevitable does arise as the book progresses, it comes more from the particular qualities of the interacting characters: they are not determined or stripped of a dimension by being forced to live in a predetermined present tense.

Abrahams specifically allows for two possibilities. One is an articulate version of the attitude to time in *Udomo* and is evoked in the character of Mhendi (whose personal situation is significantly influenced by events). At one point he meditates:

143

'These were the rules of life's game. A man could not choose where or how he was born. A man was made by the land and situation into which he was born, by the colour with which he was born. Over these he had no choice, no say of any kind. He was a prisoner. Virtue, then, or the lack of it, was in the way a man responded to his situation.'[1] This set of conclusions is specifically related to Mhendi's personal situation at a given moment in time, in relation to his past and the prospects for his future, and also in relation to other members of the group.

> Mhendi thought: They've all changed. Even Mabi. Only I am still the same. And now they are more like me. But they have power. Their problems are problems of how to build, of how to create. Only mine are still those of how to destroy. That's the difference between us now. And what a difference![2]

That the difference is to be regarded as at least partly a product of time is clear: and yet Mhendi *has* a goal, and continues, through a series of acts of choice, or 'responses to his situation', to try to achieve that goal. Even in his pessimism he considers that men are able through choice to behave virtuously or otherwise, within the circumscriptions of their condition, one of which is the relationship between past and present. The way Mhendi reaches this conclusion and the way in which he acts upon it, constitute his 'character'. Since there are many possible conclusions arising out of his situation, his behaviour is evidently not predetermined; though each choice is conditioned by his 'character', which is in turn affected at any time by certain variables, among which the influence of past events and awareness of future prospects are always to some degree present. Mhendi sees himself as the most static of characters, and his view of life is decidedly pessimistic: yet within the limits set by himself he is, perhaps unwittingly, triumphant, and he develops in the time framework of the novel from a tendency to self-pity and drink to considerable courage and steadfastness in the face of great odds. Thus the final validity of his con-

---

[1] *A Wreath for Udomo*, p. 279. [2]*Ibid.*, p. 279.

clusions, however perspicacious these may be, is left open to doubt: it may be argued that it is belied by his own actions.

If the dominant emotional qualities of Mhendi's character are resignation and love, those of Michael Udomo may be described as restless optimism and the desire to love. The contrast between their attitudes to time, which is an important cause of tension in the book, should be seen in terms of this difference in character. Udomo's view, as we have seen, is revealed most vividly when he is confronted with his destiny, in his justification of his 'betrayal' to Selina and Adebhoy just before they have him assassinated.

There is another ironic occasion when he reveals a penetrating glimpse of his development to Mhendi whom he is about to betray to the whites of Pluralia for the sake of his vision.

> 'Trying to fool a lot of people. Fighting against time. But I'm beginning to see the shape of things. . . .'
> 'All I need is time', Udomo said in a faraway, musing tone. 'Just time.'
> 'How much?'
> 'Ten years. Five at a pinch; but ten to do it comfortably. . . .'[1]

Udomo sees man as the conscious agent, changing his environment in a race with time, the other and greater agent of change. It is evident to the reader that Udomo has created himself through his vision, has structured his environment within the framework of time, aware of the latter force as both obstacle and ally. Thus, though he may be too late to save himself, in the long run his enemies are also, in his own words, 'too late'. It is only in personal relationships that this view fails Udomo completely, in ironic contrast with Mhendi, whose philosophy in this sphere serves him perhaps too well.

Udomo is seldom seen from within: his character is revealed through the perceptions of Lois, Mabi and Mhendi. On the rare occasions when he speaks, as it were, for himself, it is

---

[1] *Ibid.*, pp. 275–6.

usually in the form of introspection, and his moments of direct self-revelation to other characters are usually accompanied by some horrible irony. When he speaks frankly to Mhendi, he is about to betray him; when he reveals his motives to Adebhoy and Selina he is at the point of betrayal himself. Other people, especially Lois, try to make contact with him, but such contact is fatal to the relationship.

The problem is a familiar one in the modern novel, and arises out of the characteristically liberal stress on the individual. In *A Wreath for Udomo* there seems to be a connection between action and isolation, which is an interesting link between two of the most typical preoccupations of liberals in and out of fiction.

Michael Udomo's life ends in complete isolation; Mhendi, who is passive and has action forced on him, has no difficulty in inspiring affection and even love, or in returning these emotions. This link is further developed in *This Island Now*, in which Josiah, the revolutionary leader, is in the end completely cut off not only from the people whose lives he seeks to change, but from his loyal and politically conscious supporters as well.

The isolation of Udomo is conveyed by presenting him indirectly through other characters, and never really allowing him to be the centre of consciousness. The difficulty here lies in the unwillingness with which one accedes to the validity of the perceptions of characters whose own features are stereotyped and whose own judgments are clichés appropriate to the stereotypes they represent. Abrahams is striving to make a very valid and important point about people in Udomo's historic situation, but his novelistic technique is insufficiently developed: Udomo remains hollow to the reader. The dilemmas and ironies which beset his existence are managed competently enough, but dilemmas and ironies alone do not constitute character. Nor is it enough simply to follow Mhendi's formula and supply the reader with information about the way Udomo responds to these complexities: that, according to Mhendi, is only a measure of virtue, and character amounts to something rather more than virtue in the modern novel. Even the perceptions of Lois are inadequate, perhaps especially so; for she, who represents the best that liberal values have to offer in ordinary living, is particularly cliché-bound, an illustration of Abrahams' constant difficulty with female characters, and, much as the reader might wish to accept the assessments of such an attractive cliché, there are no compelling grounds, from a technical point of view, for doing so.

Even if Abrahams is aiming precisely at a certain quality of elusiveness, he succeeds for the wrong reasons. Udomo is elusive because of the difficulty the other characters (through whom we perceive him) have in making moral judgments about him. One comes back to the ugly realization that character is not the same as the individual's balance sheet of virtue: if the secondary characters were more substantial we would have more to go by.

This difficulty with secondary characters plagues Abrahams' work, because of his fatal attraction to the cliché. In *Udomo*, where character is dominant, it is a serious shortcoming. To illustrate the problem, take the case of Paul Mabi. It is clear that to Abrahams the moral perceptions of an artist are in some undefined way more valid than those of ordinary people, and his relationships more sensitive and meaningful. He takes his Mabi-stereotype and enlarges it to become the hero in *A Night of Their Own*, where the magic connotations of being an artist assume over-riding importance. And yet this kind of belief rests substantially on cliché. The personal relations and moral perceptions of artists may appear to be more deeply-felt or more valid than those of less sensitive beings, but there can be no final demonstration that this must be so, nor is the evidence very convincing, since it derives from common preconceptions based on external appearances: eccentricity of dress and manners, irregularity of working hours, in other words a superficial rejection of social norms. In a criminal or a parasite the same external manifestations of nonconformity would be condemned. The point is that a novelist must be prepared to go to the trouble to convince his audience thoroughly that a character is highly sensitive and morally percipient on the basis of his behaviour as a human being, not simply on the basis of some authorial system of shorthand. Mabi might have been an agricultural implements salesman and had the same moral vision.

Some minor successes are indisputable. Lanwood is one of these: the inflexible parroting of the theoretician gone sterile combines convincingly with the sense of personal emptiness and failure which culminates in his inability to come to terms with Africa. It should nonetheless be remembered that however freshly from life Lanwood was taken, his character closely resembles a liberal stereotype, which may partly explain Abrahams' success with him. (He is said to be modelled on George Padmore.)

Selina is more problematical. The difficulty here has been encountered before in Abrahams' work and continues to recur. It may well be that Abrahams' ambivalence towards strong female characters needs to be interpreted in terms of his own psychic experience—indeed, it seems positively to invite Freudian inspection. But we are content to note the literary consequences of the phenomenon, which are embarrassing in their very predictability, apart from the structural and other infelicities they cause. Selina is a powerful market trading woman, 'tall and impassive', whose face softens only when she gives suck to her child before Udomo's gaze (which is rather startled to judge from the tone of the description). She has a mysterious control over the market traders which is never described, and provides vital assistance to Udomo's nationalist movement in its early stages. She becomes the most powerful member of the party and is instrumental in Udomo's assassination. She also acts as a procuress to the party leaders, finding women for Udomo and Mhendi but not for Lanwood, because he is 'white for all his black skin,' the result according to Selina, of having lived with a white woman for twenty years. She is meant to represent all that is—to Abrahams—evil and repressive about tribalism and traditionalism, and is endowed with symbolic force in this respect. But at the same time there is a possessive, almost caressing motherliness about her; she is a source of nourishment to the early stages of the revolution in the same way as she nourishes her baby at her breast. Of course, since the revolution is in a sense her baby, she must have the moulding of it, too: and this is the danger of all over-possessive mothers!

As the foregoing might suggest, her character is a strange combination of realism, symbolism, sentiment and balderdash, catalysed by a red-hot sector of the author's subconscious. Does Abrahams really imagine such a formidable creature defeated or rendered irrelevant by 'progress', as Udomo suggests is the case, in the last scene of the novel? The trouble is that Selina is simply not human enough to be imagined in defeat. The brilliant effect that Chinua Achebe achieves with the sudden arrest of Okonkwo by the white man in *Things Fall Apart*[1] would be impossible to realize with Selina, despite her broad similarity of outlook to Okonkwo as a traditionalist and tribal politician.

Thus it is difficult to take her seriously on the level of realism: writing from the point of view of the liberal sceptic, Abrahams is asking us to believe in the potency of witchcraft. He is very vague throughout on details about tribal society, though in general he attacks it with gusto. Occasionally he mentions weird practices, such as bathing one's feet in blood[2], or details ceremonies of dubious anthropological validity, but he nowhere descends to specifics. The passage quoted earlier in the chapter, in which Mhendi sees the canoeists as dehumanized units in a tribal machine, has a fantastic quality about it, and is distinctly difficult to accept or locate within a realistic framework.

This is not to accept the criticism of *A Wreath for Udomo* made in Akanji's (Ulli Beier) review of the book in *Black Orpheus*, that 'Udomo appears to be fighting against some bogus enemy' because the tribalism he objects to is 'never really described or explained'.[3] Abrahams' friend Nkrumah was en-

---

[1] C. Achebe, *Things Fall Apart*, (Heinemann, London, 1958), p. 23.
[2] *A Wreath for Udomo*, p. 242.
[3] *Black Orpheus*, no. 4, October 1958, pp. 56ff.

gaged in a bitter struggle for power against traditional tribal
authorities in the Gold Coast when *Udomo* was first published.
To accuse Abrahams of succumbing to 'the white man's myth
of the "primitive" negro' is absurd; as a Coloured liberal,
conscious of his South African background, he is concerned
to expose racial or colour exclusivity wherever he finds it. That
he finds the tribe a disturbingly closed and exclusive unit is clear
from his article 'The Conflict of Culture in Africa', where he
writes: 'Freedom of choice is not a prominent tribal characteristic. The tribal society is inward, exclusive, and non-demo-
cratic. Power and authority are, ultimately, concentrated in the
hands of a few. The binding oath, the secret ceremonial—
these are important!'[1] He goes on to explain that the Westernized black politician, isolated in his own country from both
white élite and tribal power structure, must enlist the latter on
his side to win his place in society. 'And in doing all these things
something happens to the detribalized man. One cannot bring
the forces of superstition and fear and darkness into play without being psychologically affected by them.' He concludes: 'To
be truly democratic the state must be founded on the underlying
assumptions of Western culture. The tribal structure served
the needs of tribal man. The moral codes of tribal man were
adequate to his time. The needs of modern man, the conditions
under which modern man lives, demand new structures and
new values. The touching love of some anthropologists for
the old ways should not blind us to their inadequacy for
modern needs. Western culture is a world culture, not "reserved
for Europeans only".' These words are sufficient to refute
Beier's accusation (and were written years before he made it),
and so declare Abrahams' own position, exactly as it is reflected
in *A Wreath for Udomo*.

Stylistically the book is occasionally subject to clichés and
picture-postcard descriptive writing, as most of his work, but

---

[1] First published in *International Affairs*, Vol. XXX, no. 3 (July, 1954)
and reprinted in *Phylon* (Atlanta University Review, Vol. 16, no. 4,
1955) p. 387.

the really awkward moments are few, which places it in the same prose period as *Wild Conquest*: a glossy woman's magazine patina has been achieved, though the subject matter is rather more serious. Of course, this has unfortunate consequences for the total effect and is always one of the crucial factors which prevents Abrahams from being as important a writer as his potential might have allowed. The sentimentality of some passages is reinforced by the easy, syrupy flow of the prose, the use of phrases worn shiny but very thin. The following passage is one of the worse examples:

> The market was old, timeless Africa; loud, crowded and free. Here, a man sat making sandals from old discarded motor car tyres; there, another worked at an old sewing machine, making a nightgown-like affair while the buyer waited; a little further on an old goldsmith worked at his dying art, but using, now, copper filings instead of gold to fashion the lovely trinkets women wear the world over; elsewhere a woman sold country cloth fashioned with such fine art that only Africans think of it as a garment of utility. Trade was slow and loud everywhere. This was as much a social as a shopping centre. For excuse to spend the day at the market a woman would walk all the way from her village to town with half a dozen eggs. She would spread them on a little bit of ground for which she paid rent. And through the day she would squat on the ground and talk to others who came for the same reason. She would refuse to sell her wares till it was time to leave. They were the excuse for her being there. There were many like that. But there were many others for whom trade was an earnest business. But, whether earnest or as an excuse, the traders were all boisterously free, loudmouthed and happy. And the laughter of the market was a laughter found nowhere else in all the world . . .[1]

It is, incidentally, a reflection of Abrahams' basically unsympathetic response to the West African environment that at moments like this his scene-setting is so crudely and obviously drawn from stock, because his evocations of left-wing Hamp-

---

[1] *A Wreath for Udomo.*, p. 148.

stead and exiled politicians in London, despite fairly frequent awkwardnesses and a very standardized manner, are much more convincing and genuine. It is, of course, inescapable that there is some degree of correlation between the class of the prose and the quality of both the thought and the feelings behind it: but at the same time, in general terms, it is impossible to question the fundamental sincerity of Abrahams' attitudes in this book, or the fact that for the first time in his novels a sustained attempt has been made to think problems through in an ordered, consequential way.

This leads us to conclude with the one undoubted and in many ways most surprising triumph of the book, which is its prophetic nature. Much was made of Chinua Achebe's *A Man of the People* because it described a military coup in Nigeria and was written a very short time before one actually took place. Achebe is no doubt the better writer, *A Man of the People* the better book, and prophecy no essential ingredient of a good novel. But *A Man of the People* is essentially predictive rather than prophetic; while *Udomo*, published in 1956 when the only independent states in sub-Saharan Africa were Ethiopia, Liberia and South Africa, not only sketches a chillingly accurate paradigm of events to come: it also assigns causes for these events, suggests their origins with some subtlety, and is understanding of human weaknesses that had not yet come into play in a situation that was not even half created. This kind of insight amounts to prophecy. Politically *Udomo* is the best thing Abrahams has ever done, and as a novel the same judgment may be made with some confidence.

7

A Night of Their Own

The interval of almost ten years between *A Wreath for Udomo* and *A Night of Their Own* seems to have offered little opportunity for development in Abrahams' art. The locale of *A Night of Their Own* is *Udomo*'s Pluralia writ large; the hero is *Udomo*'s Mabi developed a little; the plot is constituted by reality catching up with the imaginary exploits of *Udomo*'s Mhendi. And the metaphysical issue remains that of action— the characteristic liberal dilemma. In almost every respect Abrahams' ability as novelist seems no more developed that it was in the mid-'fifties; neither do his preoccupations and attitudes appear to have changed.

Like *Udomo*, *A Night of Their Own* is a political novel, prompted by actual events: the destruction of all the main branches of the liberation movement in South Africa in the twelve months from July 1963 to July 1964. The novel is dedicated, movingly enough:

For
my friends
WALTER SISULU
and
NELSON MANDELA
and all the others,
the captured and the still free,
who are at war against the evils
of this night of their own.

But it shows signs of haste (as well as emotional pressure) in construction, and perhaps as a result of these factors, it embodies the unintentional possibility of absurdity.

This is most marked by the way in which Abrahams makes every situation into a testing-ground for the postulates of what may fairly precisely be called European post-romantic liberalism. It seems at times as if the entire human race with all its relationships and interactions had been created for the purpose of testing Abrahams' creed, with the additional twist that the creed can't fail, while human beings can and do fall short of its demands.

The hero of the novel is one Richard Dube, black artist of South African origin who has spent the previous ten years Europeanizing himself in exile in Paris and London. The similarity with Mabi is clear. Dube apparently volunteers to act as courier for the beleagured South African underground movement and bring a large sum of money into the country via a submarine (presumably belonging to *someone*) for distribution among its branches and members. His sole task is to deliver the money to the right people: after that it is up to them to remove him from the scene by a secret route, so that he can, presumably, return to his easel in Hampstead or wherever. In terms of political reality, the situation is palpably improbable. What makes it the more so is Dube's apparent political quiescence during the years of his exile, since commitment to action is the living issue with him in the novel: one hopes, at least, that couriers are seldom chosen from agonizedly doubting, politically inexperienced painters.

The absurdity of Dube's situation gradually develops, and it is only at the very end of the book that the reader realizes, with a gasp of disbelief, that despite his titanic inner conflict over action and magnificent gesture of personal commitment, Dube remains, politically speaking, absolutely passive until the last. And this is despite the fact that the duration of the action is considerably lengthened by an unfortunate accident which occurs within the first hours of his return to South African soil.

He is met off the submarine by a symbolic and not untypical victim of South Africa's racial structure: an Afrikaner who, having been accepted as a white man all his life, is suddenly declared 'Coloured' by the implacable genetic bureaucracy that safeguards the world's highest standard of living. To revenge himself on the group that has betrayed him, Westhuizen becomes a link man in the underground movement's escape section. He meets or takes out incoming and outgoing underground politicians in the crucial coastal stage of their entry or exit—either the first or last lap—because a white man's company near an exposed and isolated stretch of coast makes a black man's presence that much less suspicious if he is encountered by the police: the black automatically becomes the servant of the white.

But Westhuizen's loyalties, not surprisingly, have not changed as easily as his colour category. He tells Dube (who is called Nkosi for most of the novel, this being the pseudonym that has been chosen for him):

> 'What do you expect?' Westhuizen sounded friendly. 'You yourself said I sound like one of them. That's because I am: I look like them, I sound like them, I think like them. I feel like them. Nobody and nothing can change that.'[1]

They are stopped by a police patrol during their own drive inland, and one of the two policemen evinces suspicion of Westhuizen. When the two reach their contact men, who are Indians, in the depth of a field of sugar cane, Nkosi reports his impressions:

> Westhuizen pulled up. From nowhere a figure appeared beside the car.
>   A voice said: 'Mr Nkosi...'
>   'Yes?'
>   'Good.'
>   Westhuizen said: 'This is going to cost you double. Twenty Rand, not ten. For this one and all the others.'
>   Nkosi said: 'I don't know how, but he knew what I carried. We were stopped by a patrol and I think they are suspicious of him.'
>   'Damn lying Kaffir!' Westhuizen hissed. 'The patrol wasn't

---

[1] *A Night of Their Own* (Faber and Faber, London, 1965), p. 27.

suspicious and I only guessed about the money. He gave himself away: it's him.'

There was silence, then the shadowy figure beside the car said: 'Think there'll be a follow-up?'

'What you mean, follow-up?' Westhuizen asked.

'I think so,' Nkosi said and decided that the new man sounded like an Indian. . . .

Sammy Naidoo said: 'They were stopped by a patrol.'

'Only one? I expected them to be stopped at least twice.'

'But this is the point, Doc. Mr Nkosi says Westhuizen knew about the money and that the patrol was suspicious enough to want to follow-up.'

'I know they'll follow-up,' Nkosi said. 'He was in a panic and one of them shone a torch in his face and saw it. He has to go and register me in the morning.'

Nkosi felt the sudden tension in both men.

'Didn't he give you a passbook?'

'No.'

'But I gave it to him, Doc.'

'All right, Sammy, I'm sure you did. Tell me, my friend, how do you know he knew about the money?'

Nkosi told them about the meeting with Westhuizen and repeated his words about how needed what Nkosi brought was to the opposition. Then he told them of Westhuizen's direct reference to the money and his statement about not taking it because Nkosi's friends were particularly good at painful murders.

'Yes, I see,' Nunkhoo said. 'Of course, you didn't deny it. . . .'

'When he gave the password, I assumed he was one of us.'

'Naturally. We knew this was the most risky part. Anybody else but a white man—or an apparent white man—would have been searched.'

'This route must now be closed,' Naidoo said.[1]

This last sentence of Naidoo's is the real beginning of the action of the book. Abrahams creates a situation in which every character is categorized according to the colour of his

[1] *Ibid.*, pp. 32, 33–4.

skin—a fair imitation of the South African reality. He extends this to include the underground opposition to the regime, putting the Indians in a special position. In 1949 race rioting between Zulus and Indians in Natal took place and many Indians fell victim, while the white authorities did little to intervene. Abrahams takes this as a crucial point of historic reference, to which his Indian characters—all active members of the underground—frequently return. Within the underground, they are suspected and rejected by the dominant Africanist wing; in daily life, their rejection at the hands of the ruling whites is even more final and contemptuous, and they must compete with Africans, in many situations, for the lower-level employment opportunities that are available. In addition to all this, they are the smallest group in the South African colour spectrum, though relatively populous in the province of Natal, where the novel is set. A more elaborately prepared arena for the trial of liberal values in action against human nature can hardly be imagined.

The first encounter comes soon after Nkosi, installed in the house of Dr Nunkhoo and his sister Dee (they are rich Hindus) has rested after his experiences on arrival.

> Nkosi sat down to the kind of Indian meal he had not eaten for a very long time: a feast of delicately balanced meats and vegetables, superbly flavoured with spices of which curry powder is only one. The *rôti* was as light as air and its flaky butteriness titillated the roof of the mouth.
>
> Her eyes and face softened to his obvious appreciation of the food.
>
> 'Is it only hunger or do you really like this?'
>
> 'Both. But I've never had any curry as good as this. Not even in Durban before I left. And I had a lot of it.'
>
> 'After two days without food, anything would taste good.'
>
> 'Since you must sell yourself short—yes. Have I really been out for two days?'
>
> 'A day and a night and a day.'
>
> He remembered the nightmarish journey with the white man who had been made Coloured by decree and who could not help feeling white in spite of everything.

'How much do you know about this business?'

'Which?' The softness went out of her and she became hard, alert.

'My coming here.' He thought: She knows everything about it.

'Only that you brought money for the underground.'

'Nothing else?'

'Nothing else.'

'Not even about my journey or where I came from?'

'No.'

He wondered why she found it necessary to lie, and so obviously; and why there was this strong undercurrent of resentment flowing from the woman. Perhaps it was because she was a cripple; but no one could sustain resentment that long. It would be like holding your breath till you died, except that the body would not permit it. At a certain point, the will ceases to function and the instinctive impulse to survive, to breathe in and breathe out, takes over. So this consciously felt resentment could not be something sustained over the years because she was a cripple.

The woman seemed to pick up his line of thought; a bitter, derisive, slightly contemptuous smile flitted across her face.

'You've been away a long time?' she asked.

'Yes,' he said, on guard, bracing himself. 'A long time.'

'Something like ten years, I understand?'

'That's about it,' he said and wondered: What now?

'One loses touch,' she said with a hint of rudeness, 'being away so long.'

'You're probably right,' he said curiously. 'Why?'

'I think you've lost touch,' she said.

Oh dear, he thought, she's going to make a scene: but why?

'As you say,' he said. 'Ten years is a long time.'

'And without being aware of it one adopts the values, attitudes, thought-patterns of the society in which one finds oneself.'

All right, he thought: I'll meet you halfway.

'What are you trying to say?'

'That it's premature for you to judge us, because you're out of touch with your own country and might judge it by the flabby moralistic standards of the middle class Europeans among whom you've spent so much of your life.'[1]

This is the beginning of a relationship which revolves around the question of commitment. Dee is committed to the struggle because of the cruelty of her first lover, a left-wing white fellow student at LSE years before: because of her fear of personal relationships which arises out of that experience: because of her distaste for a system of values that lays emphasis on the importance of the individual, since it is her individuality that has been hurt within such a system. She is committed despite— or, again, because of—certain shortcomings in her world view, which emerge in her reactions to Nkosi:

> For the first time, immediately, startlingly, the woman saw him as an individual person, a man. Up to this point he had been, like all other Africans—like all white people, like all Coloureds— a representative: a person representing and symbolizing this or that racial group.
>
> It is because I hurt him, she thought: he's sitting across the table and I can see the pain in his eyes and almost feel him feel it. Would I have behaved like this if he were white, or even Coloured? Is it the race and colour thing again? But the whites and the Coloureds haven't done to us what the Africans have, not directly at least. How responsible must he be for his people? How responsible am I for what my people do? . . .
>
> Then after a long while of silence, she said in a tentative, conversational voice: 'You do sound like the Europeans, you know.'
>
> He thought: Perhaps we'll get on better now; it's worth a try anyway.
>
> 'Sound or behave?'
>
> 'But then I was a bit like that too when I came from Europe,' she added, ignoring his question.
>
> 'Like what?'
>
> 'Like you are. Uncommitted, detached, objective—any of those words would do: you know what I mean.'

[1] *Ibid.*, pp. 44–6.

We progress, he told himself.

'So, being European is being uncommitted, detached, objective?'

'You are deliberately distorting my meaning now. What I really mean is that you react and respond with the kind of self-assurance that is not common to us—all of us—who are non-Europeans in this country.'[1]

The weakness of her position is clearly demonstrated: incidentally, if not inevitably, it reflects the shortcomings of Abrahams' historical perspective, because in this novel (as in *A Wreath for Udomo*) one of the authorial preoccupations is some notion of African 'guilt', in this case arising specifically out of the 1949 Zulu-Indian race riots. The usual contradiction is present here: why this, as a symbolic situation instancing the characteristic shortcomings of group thinking and behaviour, should also be connected with the strangely persistent notion in Abrahams' work that Africans as a group are in some way 'guilty',[2] is difficult to understand.

Nkosi's initial view of commitment is what leads Dee to comment that he is 'uncommitted, detached, objective':

> She lowered her head and said: 'I'm sorry, Mr Nkosi. I had no say in your coming to this house, no choice in your being here. No business. . .'
>
> 'Nor I,' he said. 'And the sooner I can leave the better I'd like it. The job is done; there's nothing to keep me here now.'[3]

Clearly each is meant to represent an extreme on the anti-oppression continuum: Nkosi that of liberal uncertainty—as he himself puts it,

> 'The point is to accept being uncertain, to accept being afraid, even to entertain the possibility of disaster and still to carry on. We must cultivate self-doubt and introspection in order to remain human.'[4]

[1] *Ibid.*, pp. 46–7.

[2] cf. *A Wreath for Udomo*, p. 121

[3] *A Night of Their Own*, p. 47.

[4] *Ibid.*, p. 52.

and Dee, that of total commitment, to the point of complete self-sacrifice. Through their relationship each becomes healthier, more capable of self-recognition. Nkosi's sceptical commitment to individuality becomes a devoted commitment to an individual, and Dee's devoted commitment to Africans as a cause becomes a much more fundamental commitment to an individual person who happens to be an African.

The plot of the novel might be seen as perfunctory, a gesture in the direction of the efficient political thriller, so saturated is the action with the reiteration of the standard liberal ideas and dilemmas about action expressed in none too successful dialogue. (To coin an aphorism, Abrahams' people talk like characters in a novel.) But it possesses a significant level of organization which makes its contribution to the total complex of meaning. This consists in the way all events and characters are so structured as to exist in a continuing state of reaction to Nkosi-Dube, the paradoxically passive central character, who arrives, performs his absurdly simple mission of handing over a packet of money, and simply waits in hiding while others tempt death in their efforts to get him safely back where he came from. Nkosi's passivity is actual only on the ostensible level of the plot. But his mere presence in South Africa leads to the murder of Westhuizen, a series of nationwide manhunts by the security police, the killing in police headquarters of Sammy Naidoo, the tough trade unionist who is also in love with Dee, the collapse of the relationship between Carl Van As, brilliant Afrikaner career civil servant whose job it becomes to track down Nkosi, and his Coloured mistress, and Van As's final surrender to moral corruption. Nkosi is also responsible for the healing of Dee's psychic wounds, the political reconciliation between the Indian commercial magnate, Old Man Nanda, and his son Joe, and the emergence of a morale-building myth among the masses of an indestructible opponent of oppression called Richard Nkosi, a convenient identity to be used by the underground movement whenever the need arises.

Nkosi-Dube's catalytic function can be compared to the injection of a potent antibiotic into a diseased organism. Every part of the organism reacts, the agents of the disease most strongly. But does the disease-destroying drug undergo changes in its nature during this process?

The weapon that Nkosi-Dube carries (to vary the metaphor) into the South African struggle is, as he himself suggests, the characteristic two-edged liberal blade of uncertainty and self-doubt. This soon gets him into trouble with Dee, who is committed despite the fact that she saw her brother killed by Africans on her return to South Africa in the 1949 riots; and with Sammy, whose commitment is complete, so that he arranges the killing of Westhuizen, the suspect link man.

Naidoo spread his big hands on the desk top and stared at them.

'I'm sorry but your end of the arrangement has broken down.'

'Westhuizen?' Nkosi asked.

Naidoo nodded.

'How? Did he talk?'

'No. He didn't talk, but they found the passbook he should have given to you. They also found out pretty quickly who he was.'

'The patrol people knew him as Coetzee.'

'They—and the whole country—now know that Coetzee is Westhuizen. It's on the radio and all the papers have it, and the story of how he was declared Coloured a year ago.'

'Poor brute,' Nkosi said. 'But he'll talk, you know.'

Naidoo raised his head and looked directly at Nkosi.

'He won't. He's dead.'

Nkosi looked at Dee and knew that she had known all along. She stared back at him, stony eyed, and it was as though he heard her voice say: I told you out there is evil.

'Who did it? The police or . . .'

You're quick, Naidoo thought, too damn quick.

'He could lead them to Sammy and you,' Dee said, a harsh flatness to her voice.

'And so he had to go. . . .'

'What else?' she asked. . . .

Dickie Naicker's funny jazz, Naidoo told himself.

'What right have we—'

'The right of necessity, of history, of survival,' Naidoo cut in quietly. 'It is either that or we all submit all the way.'

Nkosi shook his head violently but spoke quietly.

'I'm not talking about an uprising or sabotage or a revolution. This is the straightforward and simple murdering of one man, a poor brute who helped us, too.'

'Approve or disapprove, we did what had to be done.' Naidoo closed his eyes and pursed his lips. He fought down the angry words that choked him. He could not quite hide the bitterness he felt, and Nkosi felt it all the more forcefully for being controlled. 'I am responsible for what was done. I assume the responsibility.'

A wave of anger surged up inside Nkosi.

'And that, I suppose, is that.' . . .

'You will forgive me but I'm not prepared to debate the morality or the ethics of this matter now. Perhaps in another place and under different circumstances, but not here and now. So you think what you like; for us, at present, it does not matter. We can't allow it to matter.' . . .

'What does affect you,' Naidoo went on, 'is the fact that the passbook intended for you was found. For reasons of their own, they have not made this public. All they've let out is that Westhuizen was murdered by *Poqo*. But they've made hundreds of prints of the picture on the passbook and these have gone to the police all over the country.'

'They think I murdered him. . . .'

'The internal police report is that he was last seen in the very early hours of Monday morning with "a Native" and he told the police patrol that he had picked up "the Native" on the Protectorate border. The order is to get this "Native" at all costs and to get him alive. But the published reports of the death of Westhuizen have none of this.'

Naidoo paused, half expecting Nkosi to speak. Some of the weariness and hunger in him showed on his face. . . .

'How do you know all this?'

To Naidoo he sounded remarkably calm. Dee felt the knotted tension in him. An odd flicker of feeling passed over Naidoo's face.

'My brother, my elder brother, is a Detective Sergeant in the Political Division.'

'I see,' Nkosi said.

Naidoo's control suddenly went.

'You do, do you! What the hell do you see, Mister?'

'Sammy, please,' Dee said.

'It's all right,' Nkosi said to Dee.

'It's all right,' Naidoo mimicked with rising anger. 'The man says it's all right; so it's all right; the man says he sees so he sees. He's wise, he's civilized, he doesn't like murder and he sees. Well, let me tell you something, Mister. You may be black and you may be born here but you don't see a damn! In fact, I'm sick of your little-Lord-Jesus attitude!'

'Sammy!' This time Dee was angry. 'Mr Nkosi's our guest!'

'*Yours*, not mine or ours!' Sammy snapped. Then he pulled himself together and shook his head. 'I'm sorry, Dee. I didn't mean that. It's just that he seems to refuse to understand. . . .'[1]

Nkosi's attitude undoubtedly appears, from one point of view, indefensibly holier-than-thou, and the weaknesses of undiluted European liberalism are exposed by the situation. But Dee's suspicion and Sammy's rigid refusal to reopen issues that have been long decided for him do not necessarily constitute an adequate response to the situation either. Some sort of pollination must take place, and it is symbolically achieved in the love affair which develops between Nkosi and Dee.

There is not much action in this either: Nkosi-Dube is a still point at the storm's center. They come together and make love a few times: Dee uses the opportunity of purging the sex-based racial jealousy felt by Dicky Naicker, Sammy Naidoo's young protégé who is attending on Nkosi in hiding. The positive issue of the affair for the participants bodes well, symbolically, for the future of their joint political struggle, but a hard time ahead is indicated by their parting, with Nkosi's successful escape, at the end of the book. For Dee, the change that has been wrought in her is demonstrated structurally. She returns to Durban Point, where years ago she had seen her brother murdered by blacks, this time to watch out of sight the steamer that is secretly carrying her remaining brother and her black lover to safety.

---

[1] *Ibid.*, pp. 57–9.

In Nkosi's case the nature of the commitment has to be defined verbally, since words are also the weapons of the sceptic. He produces this definition when he is challenged by Old Man Nanda, the reactionary Indian millionaire. Nkosi and Dr Nunkhoo, Dee's brother, are being hidden from the security police by Nanda's son in the family house, which is probably above suspicion for a while because of Old Man Nanda's loyalty to the government that oppresses his fellow-Indians. Nanda asks what must seem to many ordinary South Africans two crucial questions:

'. . . But tell me, how you think you going to get rid of this government that has all the power in its hand?'

'I think you're asking the wrong man, father. Ask me.'

'I already asked you, Joe—remember? You told me it was a thing of time, a thing in which many people, including my own son, is likely to die. So I ask him because I hear they say he cannot be caught and he cannot die. Why must other people, why must my people, my son, an Indian doctor, die for you and your people?'[1]

Nkosi's response is instructive.

'. . . Now sir, I can die and I can be caught and it may yet happen. What we do not want to happen—all three of us, and all the people in the movement against *apartheid*— what we do not want to happen is for the *idea* represented by Richard Nkosi to be destroyed. My name isn't really Richard Nkosi. I have just borrowed the name, as others have before me, and as others will after me, because the name has now been turned into the spirit and the will of the resistance. It is a symbol now.'

'And if they catch you?'

'They will be able to identify me, myself, my own person, with Richard Nkosi, because they have evidence to show that it is I who have been using that name. And they will also be able to prove my real identity as a man. So two things will happen: the myth will be destroyed and in the process the hope

[1] *Ibid.*, p. 248.

for victory on which the spirit of resistance feeds will be shattered for a long time to come, for many generations perhaps.'

'And it is for this fairy story that you take these risks?'

'No, sir. It is for the people of this country, but primarily it is for what I believe. I think this is the difference between ourselves and other animals.' . . .

'So now we all believe in fairy stories!' the old man scoffed.

'But indeed we do.'

'The killing of Indians by your people, and the brutality of the white people, and the hatred all over this place, is this your magic world of fairy stories! Till now you talked sense, young man, even though I did not agree with you. But now . . . This is dreaming!'

'Yes,' Nkosi said slowly after a while. 'This is dreaming.'

Inwardly, he gave the old man best, and the other three sensed it. The old man had insisted on this encounter and had come out best. . . .

The old man felt his sense of triumph ebb away. The three young men had shown they recognized that he had scored a point, but they were unimpressed. Why?

'So your risks are foolish,' he said a little more aggressively than he intended.

'I don't agree,' Nkosi said. 'To agree with you that this is dreaming is not to agree with you that dreaming is foolish. If you think it is foolish, then it is foolish to you. It is not to us.'

'Then show me the sense of it!' the old man said impatiently.

'I'm not sure I can. How can I make you understand why looking at a flower makes me feel good? I can't even explain it to myself. I can use words like beauty, scent; but why do I respond to these things as I do? I don't know. All I know is that I do. I don't even know what this conscious life within me is. All I know is that I'm alive, and being alive I, and others like me, have felt the need, generation after generation, to affirm and reaffirm, again and again, the inviolability of the human spirit— this thing that makes us feel tender and angry and makes us love and believe in abstractions like dignity and justice and good.

'You've just shown there is ugliness. I don't know how to explain that either. But I know it is there and I know that what I describe as the need to affirm the inviolability of the human spirit may at critical times demand that we fight to the death against this ugliness. Ours is not the first generation called upon, and I don't think it will be the last. This is our responsibility now, because in our time the greatest ugliness in the world and the greatest danger to the human spirit is here in our land. And this has nothing to do with race or colour. The sense of it? I don't think everybody in the movement agrees with me; I don't agree with much that is in the movement; and heaven knows I have done very little compared with others. But the sense of it is that the great South African adventure, that intense and special dialogue between the people and the earth which shapes and fashions and nurtures them, can only begin when the land is rid of this racial ugliness. This must be done before there can be any real beginning.'[1]

The immediate result of this peroration is that Old Man Nanda agrees to help the two fugitives escape, and approaches the upright Scandinavian skipper of a vessel belonging to a company that trades with him, successfully persuading him to spirit them out of the country. And then the Old Man has a (fortunately mild) heart attack.

The content of Nkosi's climactic declaration of commitment obviously comes out of his experiences from the moment of being landed on the South African coast; in terms of overt action, as has been suggested, these do not amount to very much. Love is the name that leads him to accept the shirt of fire which is commitment to action for the liberal sensibility; the only thing that happens to him is his falling in love with Dee Nunkhoo, and it is this relationship that leads him to the grand-sounding declaration of the existential need 'to affirm and reaffirm, again and again, the inviolability of the human spirit'.[2] But as an intellectual climax (which is surely the intention), this passage, though it gives off a fine ring, echoes its emptiness in the end. The liberal pessimism which saw self-doubt as a virtue, as a sound instrument for testing the experiential world, was perhaps equally banal, but it at least possessed a degree of coherence. Nkosi himself admits the difficulty of communicating his new existential commitment.

---

[1] *Ibid.*, pp. 248–52.　　　　　　[2] *Ibid.*, p. 251.

And in fact it is all very unsatisfactorily vague.

> '. . . the sense of it is that the great South African adventure, that intense and special dialogue between the people and the earth which shapes and fashions and nurtures them, can only begin when the land is rid of this racial ugliness.'[1]

The rhetoric is almost convincing, for a moment: but re-examination shows that there is no core, that the 'sense' is absent from the sentence. The climax suffers a collapse into the banality of the surrounding fictive landscape. The real liberal dilemma of action dissolves, rather than resolves itself, into a fizz of fine words.

Although this is a specific failure, its roots are in the texture of the novel as a whole. And in fact they go deeper than that, into an attitude which has been evident in Abrahams' work from as early as *Wild Conquest* (1952), though at that time it certainly cut across the expressed grain of his ideological preferences. In *Udomo* it was much more overt, and was one of the composite elements of the attack on 'tribalism', the real provenance of which has been examined in a previous chapter; and in the last two novels it constitutes a veritable astigmatism in Abrahams' world view.

In *A Night of Their Own* the attitude emerges in the heavy dependence on stereotype in dealing with minor characters, especially non-white ones; the immensely patronizing tone in the conversation between Nkosi and Dicky Naicker, at the Nunkhoo's upcountry farm, where Nkosi has been taken for concealment by Naicker (this episode is worth a closer look), and in passages like this one:

> *And in all the dark places of the land the word went out that the battle was on and that everyone had to be calm and peaceful: no one should resist arrest, no one should fight back, but no one should co-operate. In this phase the battle was between the hunters and the hunted. And everybody knew who the hunters were and everybody knew that the hunted was and is and will be Richard Nkosi until the*

---

[1] *Ibid.*, pp. 251–2.

battle is over and victory is won. . . . And this was the word to spread. The time for a different form of battle would come soon enough: for now, this was the battle-order.

The word spread until it too was nationwide like the arrests; whispered from man to man, from woman to woman, passed on even from child to child till, in the end, it reached up to the highest places in the land.[1]

Or this one:

He went out of the room without replying. The passage and the waiting-rooms were still crowded. It seemed that suddenly all of Dr Nunkhoo's patients had become ill and needed attention. But Van As knew it wasn't as simple as that. It was one of those group things with which he had become familiar. Whatever the time of night or day, whenever some important leader was being taken or questioned or hunted for, the group would be there, appearing from nowhere and everywhere. And it had a very distinct presence, hard to pin down, hard to define, but forcefully real. And it was this that had led many a policeman to jumpy and stupid action often resulting in the outbreak of unnecessary violence and rioting. He felt the presence of the group now, all about him, not hostile but assertive, ensuring that he understood its nature and purpose, which was to warn of the hidden forces behind the wanted leader and that those forces would protect his loved ones and the things that are his.[2]

The extracts suggest various explanations, or excuses; authorial laziness is one, a striving after an unfamiliar atmospheric effect is, perhaps, another. A third possibility is that the sheer unreality with which the situations, highly unlikely ones in themselves, are depicted, suggests a barrier between Abrahams and precisely those people on whose behalf, in a sense, this book and most of his novels have been written. This last attempt at diagnosis is perhaps confirmed by the detailed inspection of what happens when Nkosi broaches theoretical subjects with young Dicky Naicker, who has just guided him to relative

---

[1] *Ibid.*, p. 203.　　　　　　　　　　[2] *Ibid.*, pp. 207–8.

safety, in an admirably practical manner, on the Nunkhoo's isolated farm. Nkosi has asked him what he thinks the fate of the Indians in South Africa will be 'when we defeat the Nationalists', and the conversation develops naturally into a general discussion of racial feeling.

'It is the same as anything else: only thing is the colour bar hits us from two sides and that rough sometimes. But if we show the Africans we are on their side things may be better later.' . . .

'Also,' Dicky Naicker said with a hint of self-consciousness, 'all prejudice is bad. . . . Sammy says so.'

'Cissie says we're all born with prejudice and it will never change.'

The corners of Dicky Naicker's mouth turned downward, he hunched his shoulders, bent his back a little, cocked his head slightly to the right, and raised both hands, palms up, in one of the most characteristic of all Indian gestures—a gesture part supplicatory, part defensive, and wholly humble.

'I don't know: maybe Cissie right, maybe Sammy right; maybe prejudice will never change. I don't know. Maybe it's just bad to be a char in this land.'

'Char?' Nkosi queried.

'Char . . . coolie . . . Indian. All the same.'

'But we must go on,' Nkosi said.

'Yes, sir. That what the doc and Sammy say. You think it will finish one day?'

'One day,' Nkosi said.

'I mean for us too. You know what I mean, sir.'

'I think so; for you too.'

'You know, sir, it's the first time I'm talking like this to . . .'

'To a black man?'

'Yes. It really free over there, in England?'

Yes, let us change the subject, Nkosi thought. 'Yes. It's free. But there's prejudice.'

'Just like Cissie say?'

So we're not running away from it after all, he thought: bully for your movement. This conversation at this place, at this time is ridiculous.

He said: 'Cissie's wrong, Dicky. There is nothing in the world that never changes. Everything changes. Life is change.'

'That's what Sammy tell us all the time.'

'But change could be bad as well as good.'

'I know what you mean, sir.' The young Indian was very sober, very adult, very responsible. 'Like I told you, we talk about it in the movement: we understand.'

Yes, Nkosi thought, you have to; even if you cannot express it clearly. He got up from the table and found his way to the bedroom. . . .

In the kitchen Dicky Naicker rinsed the cups and the teapot; he filled the pressure stoves with kerosene and wiped them clean; then he found a clean tablecloth and laid the table for one. All this done, he went into the front room, checked doors and windows, and only then did he go to bed in the smaller bedroom. Unlike Nkosi, he did not fall asleep instantly. . . . A series of images, rather than thoughts, raced and chased through his mind, crowding each other this way and that, like over-excited children at play: Miss Dee gripping the little black man's hands and begging; Sammy Naidoo looking at her and Miss Dee looking that same way at the little black man; and the brain of the little black man working just like the clock he opened once to see how beautifully it ran . . . tick-tock-tick-tock-tick-tock-tick-tock-tick-tock . . . Smooth and easy. The picture of the clock and the picture of the little man's face merged . . . tick-tock-tick-tock . . . And Miss Dee and him doing that thing because she want to . . . tick-tock-tick-tock . . . And the face of Sammy wanting Miss Dee like she want him . . . tick-tock . . . Life is change. . . .

Then, images juggled themselves into a single clear thought: *if* this one led the underground, *if* this one ruled after the whites, then things *would* be better; change, then, would be good. . . . Comforted by this thought, Dicky Naicker resolutely put the images out of his mind, turned on his side, closed his eyes, and waited patiently for sleep to come.[1]

One is led to question the authorial assumptions that seem to underlie this passage. Why shouldn't Dicky Naicker

---

[1] *Ibid.*, pp. 112–14.

be capable of thoughts, rather than 'a series of images . . . like over-excited children at play'? Why should he be unable to express himself clearly on this subject which so closely affects his daily life? Why should he be so intellectually passive, a willing audience for Nkosi's rather irritating (in the circumstances) and highly conventional wisdom?

Again, when Joe Nanda and the courier Isaacs meet, for the latter to hand on the instructions of the Central Council regarding the fate of Nkosi, who is hiding in the Nanda house, the major factor in their considerations is rather an odd one:

> 'Thing to remember is that, if we don't get him out by tomorrow night, the risk of his getting caught will be increased a thousandfold and, if he's caught, the value of the Nkosi myth will be destroyed forever.'
> 'And we suffer a major defeat.'
> 'As you say,' the little man named Isaacs said. 'A major defeat.'[1]

The widespread belief among the black masses in the 'Nkosi myth' seems, inevitably, whichever way you look at it, to constitute a weakness rather than a strength, basic questions of credibility apart; why does Abrahams turn it into the central issue?

Obviously, Abrahams' attitude to the 'masses', the bulk of the ordinary, oppressed Africans, Indians and Coloureds in South Africa, is from a strictly literary point of view both patronising and unreal, characterized by an immense feeling of distance. The 'masses' apparently inhabit a different planet from Nkosi, Dee, Sammy, Van As, Joe Nanda and Isaacs: a planet on which the same criteria of objective reality do not apply. If this is what Abrahams really feels, that the level of life and perception possessed by the 'masses' is somehow qualitatively different from that of the narrow élite who constitute the 'characters' of his novels, what is the purpose of the kind of action he describes and explicitly approves of in *A Night of*

---

[1] *Ibid.*, p. 243.

Their Own? Logically, if the 'masses' think and feel differently from Nkosi-Dube and company, the latter are debarred from any conclusions about the kind of life the 'masses' *should* lead, or be allowed to lead; and thus all political action of this kind is nullified at its source.

A Night of Their Own constitutes something of a special case in Abrahams' development, the direction of which follows the classical post-World War II Western pattern. This is a movement from decisive involvement with mass political deprivation and action to equally decisive withdrawal from and rejection of almost all kinds of action, and emphasis on a mystique of individuality which is a sort of decadent romantic (and essentially élitist) loneliness. The specific situation of *A Night of Their Own* taken in conjunction with Abrahams' biographical relationship to it leads to a surface commitment to the idea of political action which contradicts the decisive direction of his development. Thus his evocation of any kind of action on the level of the ordinary, undifferentiated man in the mass is bound to be at least unconvincing, at worst insincere. The basic rejection of ordinary humanity triumphs over the artificial necessity for commitment to action demanded by the South African situation. That is why Nkosi, around whom the problem of action revolves, never undertakes any. Of course the dichotomy is false: between the mass and the individual there is continuity, not a chasm. Abrahams participates fully in the historic confusion of bourgeois Western artists of our day. In his next novel, his most recent up to now, this confusion becomes complete.

8

This Island Now

This Island Now may be regarded as a culminative step in the latest stage of Abrahams' development. In it the author seems preoccupied with the need to define as clearly as possible the outlines of the social and political philosophy which he has been in the process of adopting since the early 'fifties. The book is, perhaps, better constructed and less hastily written than its immediate predecessor, and is not so closely tied to a specific real situation, which partly explains why its conclusions contradict those of *A Night of Their Own*, published only a year earlier. There is not much doubt that *This Island Now* constitutes the more genuine expression of Abrahams' world view. Set in a Caribbean island, it exploits a familiar scenario, one which deviates little from that used in *A Wreath for Udomo*. The opportunity for political transformation is offered, in this case by the death of the venerable, corrupt but charismatic President, Moses Joshua. His successor, Albert Josiah, is 'a man of the people', self-made, immensely able, altogether dedicated to changing the power structure of the island, to shifting the centre of gravity from the white descendants of slave-owners, the Creole aristocracy and the expatriate businessmen, to the 'little people', the impoverished, intimidated and servile black majority.

The major difference between this novel and *A Wreath for Udomo*, in terms of the issues involved, is the emphasis laid on race and colour as historical determinants of political and personal behaviour. In *A Wreath for Udomo*, Abrahams, at his prophetic best, foresaw the political difficulties that lay in store for independent Africa. It was the first application by an African of political lessons learnt from Europe to the coming experience of his own continent. Of course, race and colour do come into *Udomo*, but in general they are there in order to be de-emphasized, or exposed as irrelevant. It is arguable that even the betrayal of Mhendi is meant to support Abrahams' political thesis; it is not placed in the context of colour prejudice. And Lois's experience with Udomo again illustrates an aspect of the general political line Abrahams was then concerned to advance.

In *This Island Now* the political line of development is very much taken for granted. The political process is seen as inevitable, irreversible: what makes it more than ordinarily dangerous is the admixture of the racial factor.

This is amply evidenced by the racial spectrum covered by the book's main characters. Despite the fact that there are so many of them, they can scarcely be said to constitute a cross-section of the island's population—in itself an interesting, even vital point, which will be elaborated upon. But they include Jews both with and without a slight hint of dark pigmentation; Chinese-Negro; Anglo-Saxon; Creole; pure negro, subdivided into lighter- and darker-skinned. Thus race, in the sense of colour, is a theme: the inter-relationships of the leading characters are defined by it. They are, in nearly all cases, only marginally affected by the steadily increasing despotism of Albert Josiah, which is foreseen all along by some of the older political hands. It is true that one aspect of this process is examined with fairly close attention (though in the end some doubts are conveyed in regard to its centrality, if not its relevance): but it is an aspect that is closely tied in with the theme of race. This is the question of personal freedom, of the integrity of the individual: and the suggestion of its historic relativity marks the distance Abrahams has trodden on the post-Romantic path.

The closest thing the book has to a central character (apart from the island itself, which is as under developed from a literary point of view as it is socio-economically) is a hybrid named Martha Lee. She is part Chinese, part Negro: in physical appearance, she is 'almost completely flat-chested, and the rest of her long lean body showed only the vaguest hints of feminine curves'. She is in the tradition of Abrahams' dominant females:

she possesses more personal and political wisdom than any other character, or perhaps than all the rest put together; and altogether the effect is formidable, though free from the sinister aspect of someone like Selina in *Udomo*. By profession she is a journalist, 'Political and Diplomatic Correspondent of *The Voice of the Island*', the only newspaper; and she is involved in an affair with Joel Sterning, who has married into the Isaacs family, which controls a mercantile empire on the island. Sterning is the classic Western liberal: indecisive, agonized, paralysed into inaction by the fear of consequences. He regrets his marriage because of the unscrupulous way in which his wife's family exercises power, though he is himself a key member of the board of Isaacs Enterprises. Such a stock set of built-in contradictions do not help to make him one of Abrahams' most memorable characters: nor is his wooden pomposity a good advertisement for the particular kind of white European liberalism which he is created to epitomize. He is not a Herzog even of the remotest provinces of the Western world; like all Abrahams' characters, he entirely lacks the comic dimension.

But even he is outmatched in stilted seriosity by the ruthless didacticism of his mistress. On her return from a protracted assignment in Europe (which was imposed on her against her will by her editor, in a gloomy sort of way the least puppet-like of the characters of this book), this is the kind of brainshower to which she subjects her maidservant, whose only error was to ask:

'How was it? Over there.'

'Not like here,' Martha said thoughtfully. How do you tell a person like this of things that are outside the range of her experience? How do you make her know what it feels like to have your self-assurance and sense of humanity undermined in a thousand subtle ways by the whites among whom you were— to such a point that you were ready to deny them their humanity? 'Not at all like here, Lydia. You won't like it. It will upset you.'

'Because of the cold?' Lydia asked. 'My sister over there is always bawling about the cold.'

'That too, yes. But really because it isn't home. You know,

for us who are Coloured and who are of the western world, who live in the western world, only this chain of islands is home. Once we leave these islands we're outsiders. We're outsiders in continental America, in Europe, in Africa, in Asia. Our ancestors came from these great land masses but they are no longer home to us. And so we're outsiders even among those who look like us but who are not of these islands. I think this is true for even the white-skinned islanders. We are a new breed, a kind of outpost of the future trapped here in the twentieth century. I think we would have a sense of being insiders, of belonging, in the twenty-first or twenty-second centuries. In today's world the people of these islands of ours are, in racial terms, trapped at a point of time that is primitive, barbaric and out of joint. Another way of putting it is that we've outgrown the prevailing racial mores of the times and because we are such an infinitesimal minority this is likely to drive us mad or else to being crucified by the majority. That is why some of us want to invent and create racial problems for the islands . . . Sorry, I'm wasting time and it is late.' Lydia did not understand, but she smiled warmly and said:

'I like it when you speak so, Miss Martha.'

'Time for bed,' Martha said briskly. 'How's your boyfriend?'

'He leave me two months now.' The maid laughed happily.[1]

Martha's overseas assignment is the reward—or punishment—for being too ready to criticize the first signs of irregularity in Josiah's regime.

Martha is very free with her advice, as may be imagined. She moves from character to character, warning Andy Simpson, the brilliant young civil servant devoted to Josiah, who becomes his Presidential Secretary, of the inevitability of the political disillusion which lies ahead; instructing her formidable editor, Maxwell Johnson, that he is in need of self-examination; informing her lover that he should never have married anyone, and even, perhaps, at the end of the book, when all is beyond hope or redemption, at a big political rally after Josiah's police have shot down two hundred rioters, looking at the lonely and

---

[1] *This Island Now* (Faber and Faber, London, 1966) pp. 181–2.

frustrated president 'as his mother had looked at him, seeing and understanding the hurt and suffering he dared not admit to himself.'[1]

Within the framework of the race theme her activity is crucial; her very genetic make-up presents her as a symbol of the potential irrelevance of colour in human affairs. But the whole tendency of her existence is to demonstrate how far from being realized this potentiality is. There is a suggestion that in the end she loses Sterning because of race; in the beginning she certainly gains him because of it.

His wife was a striking woman. Without having an ounce of excess fat there was a tropical lushness about her that most men found intoxicating. She had that flawless alabaster skin that white-skinned people with a small weak strain of Negro often showed. But he had long ago learned never to refer to the touch of Negro in the Isaacs family. They were proudly Jewish but don't dare mention the slight Negro trace in them!

Once, many years ago, a social rival of the Isaacs women— Clara, her mother, and her three younger sisters—had dismissed them as the five 'crepe sole brunettes'. The hurt had gone deep but they had to wait ten years—till the family had grown rich enough—for their revenge. When it came it was terrible and complete. Because of this piece of female cattiness the Isaacs men systematically stripped the unfortunate husband of his business, took every penny he had, sold his home and threw him out on the street. In the end, broken and on the verge of being made a bankrupt, the poor man and his family had to quit the island. That was the end of all mention, any-where, of the touch of colour in Clara's family. Since that time the wealth and influence of the Isaacs has grown even greater. For Joel Sterning, the precision with which the destruction of that unfortunate family was carried out was the beginning of the end of love.

His wife had always been the brightest of the Isaacs women, the most influential with their menfolk, and he knew she had a big part in that piece of social and economic assassination.[2]

---

[1] *Ibid.*, p. 251. [2] *Ibid.*, p. 16.

In the end his wife bears him off to his beloved Europe—but not before, in the process of her struggle to win him back, his liberal sensibilities face an unexpected challenge. In the early stages of Josiah's regime, Clara and Joel entertain to dinner their old friend John Stanhope, the Presidential Secretary, an incorruptible civil servant, devoted to his country, and a member of the Creole upper class. They discuss the (to them) unpalatable political prospect opening out before them, and Joel flares out at Stanhope because the brown-skinned élite to which Stanhope belongs has, he feels, through its 'ultraconservatism', 'literally brought Josiah about'. After Stanhope leaves, Clara entices Joel to bed with her: she succeeds, partly because he fails to contact Martha Lee by telephone. But there is another, surprising factor operating in Clara's favour:

> Martha Lee's maid told Sterning her mistress was still at the paper. The telephone operator at the paper said she had left there more than an hour earlier. He gave up and put the telephone back on its cradle. He thought of undressing then changed his mind.
>
> When he returned to the living-room Clara thought: He has not reached her. And then she was startled by the realization that she was prepared to accept the fact that Joel cared for that Lee woman, had slept with her and will sleep with her again, and that she, Clara, still wanted him and was willing to do battle with that other woman for him. Briefly, she was touched with a sense of great desolation. Joel saw her desolation and it stirred ancient racial and historic memories in him. She looked more Jewish than he had ever seen her.
>
> She said, unexpectedly, humbly: 'Will you come to me tonight?'
>
> He saw her humility and said: 'Yes.'[1]

Martha's only child is pure black, but deaf and dumb: she lives in a home for handicapped children, far out in the mountains. Even her provenance is carefully accounted for, racially speaking.

---

[1] *Ibid.*, p. 123.

Martha raised her free hand and touched the child's hair, feeling its wiry kinkiness. This child's father had been all black all the way and in his blackness had completely swamped the Chinese streak Martha had brought to the creation of the little girl. He had had his fun and he had gone on, explaining to Martha, half defiantly, half appealingly, that he had to be free; telling her, and because of his fantastic charm convincing her for the moment, that all the repressed cravings after freedom of all the unfree Negroes had reached a point of culmination in his strikingly handsome black person. So he had to take what he wanted and go on. And Martha knew that somewhere in the world at this moment, in Europe or the Americas, he was taking what he wanted, and he would, after the taking, drift on to other takings. He was the kind who would get everything except the very last bit. Right at the end of the line he would be alone, probably sick and starving and with nowhere to shelter, deserted by his charm, and no woman to hold his hand. There would be a desperate loneliness to his dying. And it would be a long way from home.

The child looked up from the ants. Martha smiled and said, out aloud: 'I was thinking of your father.'

It seemed to her that the child understood and, without words, asked: Where is he?

'I don't know where he is,' Martha murmured, running her hand over the child's hair, feeling its texture with her long fingers. 'But I know he's all right. He will always be all right until the very end. And then, right at the very end, in the moment of total defeat, his black pride will see him through. His only real fault, my dear, is that he turned his back on the island: he refused to have faith in its people and that makes him a party to all that has gone wrong here. That is the only thing I will not forgive him . . .'[1]

It would not be unfair to say that Martha is obsessed by race and colour; naturally the obsession affects all her relationships. When Sterning brings her home from the airport after her overseas assignment, he asks her if she wants him to come in with her. She replies as follows.

[1] *Ibid.*, p. 82.

'No, I'm feeling ugly and racial and you deserve better.'

'Shall I come back?'

'I'll be uglier when this is done; uglier and more hateful.'

'I'll phone you later,' he said.

She touched his hand and walked towards the house and the strong savoury smell of roasting sucking-pig coming from the back of the house. Then, abruptly, she swung about and went back to where Joel was taking her luggage out of the car. She took two big bags, one in each hand.

'I think it was the racial thing that made me play the grand lady. That's why I wouldn't marry you, Joel, wouldn't take you from your Clara. I'd never be able to be bitchy or nasty to you without the fear that it might be the racial thing and that would be unbearable and you don't deserve that kind of mental block in a relationship.'[1]

The obsession is especially pronounced in her relationship with Maxwell Johnson, her boss, whose main difficulty seems to be that he was not born an islander. He has lived there many years, married an island woman (who, apart from being built on a large scale to match the gigantic Johnson, is catalogued racially in these terms: 'All the racial strains found on the island seemed to have met in Myra, and the result was not African, not European, not Asian; and though all these had gone into the making of her, the Myra that emerged was a woman totally freed of all race or colour identification!') but Myra died in childbirth after five years of marriage, long before the action of the novel begins, and the child died too, leaving Johnson bound to the island, committed to it, as he thinks, out of his own past experience. A fairly typical encounter takes place on her return from the unwanted overseas assignment Johnson had foisted on her. He arranges a welcome party, and avoids her during it, but at the end she confronts him:

Max Johnson made sure that there was always too much noise and too many people about for Martha to be able to talk to him. And when the eating and drinking were done and it was close

[1] *Ibid.*, p. 178.

on midnight, he hustled everybody out and tried to get away himself. But Martha, anticipating this, was waiting at the gate.

'Is this all there is to it, Max?'

'Yes! Did you want roses and champagne as well!'

'You know what I mean.'

'Well don't be a damn fool. You know the score as well as I do.'

'And all you have to do is supply liquor and food and everything is made right. Even the best of you whites cannot help being arrogant and patronizing with us.'

'That's nastier than I thought even you could be,' Max cut in angrily.

'Fraternize with them a little, say a few nice words, declare your belief in racial equality, marry one of them, and you have a licence to walk all over them, to use and manipulate them. I think you'll either have to be humiliated racially, as we have been, or you'll never get over the built-in racial arrogance that has been nurtured in even the best of you for centuries.'

'You're lucky you're a woman!'

'You going to let that stop you?'

There was a long, long silence, then Max sighed heavily.

'Have you done?'

'But for one thing.'

'What?'

'I know it's an impertinence on my part—sir. . .'

'I've had enough of your crap—'

'Have you sold out to Josiah? That why I had to be out of the way?'

'You listen to me—'

'Because if it does I'm not for sale. . .'

'You go to hell!'

He walked away from her.

'I'll see *you* there first!' she yelled after his receding back.

Her anger was like dry ice; her body was under control, not shaking as with hot anger. She stood there till the tail-light of his car disappeared. Then she went into the house.[1]

---

[1] *Ibid.*, pp. 179–80.

But in the end it is Martha whose commitment to the island goes deeper than Johnson's and inevitably this must be a matter of genes. Josiah gets rid of Johnson because he needs a controlled press with a black editor for its only daily newspaper. Johnson leaves the island, and though Martha is the only one to see him depart from the airport, their last meeting is also tinged with racial irritation:

He saw his baggage through the weighing, paid the excess and headed for the departure lounge where the bar would be open even this early in the morning.

... I arrived alone, with no one to welcome me: I leave alone, with no one to say God-speed. And it took nearly forty years to make this circle. Ageing is growing lonely. That is why it is sad. . .

But he was wrong. With a full five minutes to departure time still left Martha Lee came striding into the lounge. For a terrible blinding moment the great, hulking Englishman thought he would break down and weep. Then he regained control.

... Not quite the same circle; not alone. There is one to say God-speed. Not much of an upward spiral in a forty-year circle —just one hundred per cent.

Martha climbed on to the high stool beside him. He stared steadily into his glass and said: 'I'm glad you came. I was feeling bloody sorry for myself.' Then he turned his head and looked at her.

'Black coffee.' she said to the barman, then to Johnson: 'You could have decided to stay.'

'And do what?'

'Of course,' she said evenly. 'With the job gone there is nothing to stay for.'

'Except to be a spectator of the unfolding of a not pretty picture. He paid me the compliment of not offering to buy me. I was too angry to appreciate it at the time.'

'What will you do?'

'Probably blossom into the latest expert on the Caribbean.' He looked away from her and said, thoughtfully: 'You know of course that I hate to go.'

'I know.'

'I'm going among strangers; to what's become an alien place. It's like going into exile.'

A voice over the loudspeaker announced the departure of his flight. They got off the bar stools.

'The real reason why I'm going', Max Johnson said, 'is because I feel guilty. Josiah made me see it. I am part of that white crowd that was in control for so long that it could have made the necessary changes gradually. Think what we could have done with this island over the past fifty years. Then think what we did do. And if my Board had said stay and defy him, I think I would have; they didn't and for the most disreputable reasons.'

'Some may envy you your "exile",' she said coldly. 'We cannot all pack up and go.'[1]

But the point being established, or rather reinforced, is the same one that Josiah had made to Maxwell Johnson when he had informed him at the presidential palace that the island no longer needed him. This is a long and fascinating colloquy. In it Abrahams makes perhaps the fullest statement of his view of the tragic dilemma of the leaders and people of the third world. Character is not particularly relevant to it, but since Josiah does not emerge in the book (and is not meant to) as anything but a collection of political responses, what is being defined is the gap between Martha Lee on the one hand and Johnson and Sterning on the other. Josiah asks Johnson:

'Would you accept it if I said that in your statement in my office when you said that my job is to run the country and your job is to run the paper the implication was—and indeed you said it obliquely later—that in your job, in your sphere of activity, no matter how small compared to mine, your primary responsibility, like mine, like that of any good citizen, is to the society?'

'Yes,' Max said remotely, almost carelessly. 'And you are saying I do not have the same sense of responsibility to the society that you or any other good citizen have.'

<hr>

[1] *Ibid.* pp. 240–1.

'I go further: I say it's impossible. Let me illustrate it at a very elementary level. In any conflict of interests between this country and the land of your birth who would claim your first loyalty?'

'Is the question real or rhetorical?'

'Real.'

'It will depend.'

'There you are. It is as simple as that.'

'What do you expect.'

'It doesn't depend for me, or for those like me.'

'If I were in Britain editing a British paper and a British head of state asked me the same question I'd make the same answer.'

'No doubt. And you would be one of a dozen or so and for the vast majority there will be no "it depends". I think you see what I'm driving at. When you say to me "it will depend"...' Suddenly Josiah stopped walking. He tilted his head to look up at Max Johnson, then he spread his arms out, palms upward, in a gesture at once both helpless and deprecating. 'I'm not sure I can make you understand because the state of mind and what it stems from is totally alien to anything you or your people have experienced for centuries.' He let his arms drop to his sides and shrugged slightly. 'You know, I cannot say "it depends" in the way you do and mean what you mean. It does not "depend" for me in the same way it does for you. You are primarily concerned with the salvation of your individual soul. I am not that free. Between me and your kind of freedom stands a terrible wall which I and those like me cannot climb until we have achieved the salvation of our racial soul. Till then your concern about your individual soul is a rare and enviable luxury which I recognize longingly and then put behind me. Till then we cannot be individuals in the sense that you are and until we are all relations between white and Coloured must be counterfeit by definition.'[1]

The gulf being explored here is that between the Europeanized intellectual of the third world, debarred from full parti-

<hr>

[1] *Ibid.*, pp. 210–11.

cipation in the culture into which he has been educated by factors which his very education has taught him to reject as irrelevant, and the liberal intellectual from Europe or America, committed in some way to the cause of enlightenment and the growth of individualism and freedom, but unable to understand the real, though artificial barriers to full communication between himself and his third world counterpart. There seems at first to be so much common ground, such warm and wholehearted mutual acceptance: in the end, however, Abrahams seems to agree with Josiah that 'all relations between white and Coloured must be counterfeit by definition'. The idea that there is something to be striven for and attained antecedent to freedom, before the 'universal' goal of individual fulfilment, is by now repugnant to the Western liberal intellectual tradition, especially since the initial goals so often seem to involve political measures which militate against the individual or his individuality. And the fact that these goals are in practice difficult to define, or defined so badly does not help. 'The salvation of our racial soul' is the worst kind of black power rhetoric and should be recognized as such. Unfortunately, Western liberals, with their emphasis on the importance of honest communication between people, on the primacy of personal relations, the need to participate imaginatively in the experience of others, feel guilty when faced by statements like this because of their inability to succeed in their own terms with their colleagues from the third world. This guilt is part of a well-known syndrome which leads quickly to extremist or defeatist reactions. Maxwell Johnson says it himself: 'The reason why I'm going ... is because I feel guilty. Josiah made me see it.' But Abrahams presumably does not accept this framework of ideas—or at least not entirely, since the scenario ends on a familiarly chilling note, with the inevitable breakdown of the political illusions generated by Josiah, the imposition of police state legislation, the silent rejection of Josiah by his people, and in the end, a classic liberal non-assassination—this difference between the endings of *Udomo* and *This Island Now* being, of course, of less than major importance.

186

There is an ironic reversal here located in the process of Abrahams' development. Whereas in *Udomo* he was concerned to demonstrate that in politics good intentions are vulnerable to evil from outside, in *This Island Now* he shows how good intentions combined with political power inevitably get out of hand and suggests that there is no way of reversing this process once it starts.

Abrahams' method is one of compounded irony. Andy Simpson, Josiah's would-be assassin, undergoes a long preparation before he is ready for the act. This preparation consists entirely in an orthodox novelistic view of growing up. Andy matures from a position of total commitment to Josiah's policies and personality, through various experiences, the defining ones being of suffering and loss, until he is—or thinks he is—ready to become a martyr to the principles which Abrahams has shown perpetually in retreat throughout the book—and indeed, almost throughout his work—from one point of view or another—the principles of liberal humanism. Thus his final failure to pull the trigger must be seen, at its best, as the only kind of success left for the mature liberal. A devastating conclusion! Early on, just before Josiah becomes president, Andy invites Martha to a party of his supporters, where Josiah himself offers her a 'scoop' to the effect that presidential elections will be held earlier than expected. He imposes conditions on her and she is frightened by the ease with which she allows herself to accept them. Later, she warns Andy:

'Tyranny often has small beginnings, like inhibiting one journalist a little.'

'So what do we do?' he asked, and added: 'In our context, to act in the interest of the people is to offend someone, some special interest. No matter what we do, someone will cry tyranny. He said it here not so long ago. So what do we do, Miss Lee?'

'You make it sound very easy, Andy.'

'It is you who make it sound very easy; it is you who talk about the small beginnings of tyranny. Tell me how we can do a job, which I know you agree needs to be done, without soiling our hands.'

'And when you've done the job, will we have any free institution left? . . . Take me home now, please: I'm tired.'

He took her arm and they crossed the road to where he had parked his car. 'It depends', he said, 'on which are the really key free institutions. The values of free speech and free institutions are relative. There are people—not only here but all over what has become known as the third world—who will happily trade free speech and free institutions for three square meals a day, a roof over their heads and reasonable health services. Are you prepared to say they would be making such a bad trade?'

They got into the car and he drove off.

She said: 'So it's all worked out, like every other move he has made.'

'He doesn't want to interfere with the Press unless there is no other way.'

'And you and your friends back there are prepared to do whatever he wants?'

'He wants what we want; without him we can't do it, with him we can't fail. He is the spark our movement needs.'

'And you have no doubts about him? I mean you personally, Andy?'

'None whatever, Miss Lee; not one.'

Martha looked at the houses flashing by like dark shadows. It would be a crime to try to undermine this young man's faith. All that mankind has achieved thus far on earth has been based on this kind of faith. Without it very little could have been done, very little achieved. But for the gifted and the perceptive and the genuinely compassionate ones the moment of recognition of the limitation of such a faith had often been devastating, sometimes fatal. She said, softly, tenderly: 'If things ever change, Andy, try to remember this night and our conversation, and that things are never as simple and clearcut as the shakers and shapers and revolution-makers would have us believe. There are no interest-free shortcuts. If you skip a stage in one way, you pay for it in another. So if things ever change, don't let the change change what you are, and what you believe and hold dear. You

are fine the way you are, and what you're after is right both
for yourself and our people.'[1]

Martha's wisdom is often more than a little irritating,
couched as it is in such an improbable mixture of neo-biblical
stylistics and aphoristic journalese. When Andy Simpson is lying
hidden behind the telescopic sights of his rifle, waiting for
Josiah's limousine to enter them, his thoughts return to this
conversation as a point of departure. And at the crucial
moment it is his memory of Martha's words that restrains him
from action:

> *The limousine came easily round the bend in the road and through
> the sights he could see how worried and preoccupied Josiah was.
> Now! Pull the trigger! Now!*
>
> *'There are no interest-free shortcuts. If you skip a stage in one
> way, you pay for it in another.' Martha Lee had said that to him a
> long, long time ago and he had been angry with her.*
>
> *'So if things ever change, don't let the change change you and
> what you are and what you believe and hold dear.'*
>
> *Now or he'll disappear!*
>
> *'You are fine the way you are, and what you're after is right
> both for yourself and our people.'*
>
> *You are losing him! Pull now!*
>
> *Thou shalt not kill.*
>
> *Now!*
>
> *And though I have the gift of prophecy. . . .*
>
> *Josiah's limousine passed out of sight along the winding road.
> The man lowered his head over the beautiful precision instrument
> with which he could have ended so much.*
>
> *He burst out crying; he wept with the desperate abandon of a lost
> child for whom there was no comfort. A lost child alone on an island
> over which the long shadows were creeping.*[2]

*

The quality of the climax is in some ways ludicrous, of
course, and very easy to parody, and it is a matter for regret that
Abrahams' control over matters of style has not grown with

---

[1] *Ibid.*, pp. 144–6.   [2] *Ibid.*, pp. 254–5.

his development as a novelist. But the quality of impotence suffered by Andy Simpson in the end is suggestive. It implies the practical irrelevance of liberal values in action in certain situations. Perhaps this is all that it is meant to do. But it is significant that Simpson's most powerful feeling at the moment of failure is one of isolation, of loneliness. He is 'a lost child' for whom 'there was no comfort'. The gift of prophecy has enabled him to see the real complexity of things before passing judgment: this complexity precludes the possibility of executing his judgment. But it also destroys another possibility, one that is supposedly central to the liberal canon of values. This is the possibility of communication. Simpson's isolation seems complete: he can no longer face even Martha Lee, since her scornful rejection of the pass he made at her. Josiah has injured him in many ways: he has punctured his illusions, forced him to see the permanence of evil, robbed him of the girl he wanted to marry by arresting her father, the island's chief justice, who refused to comply with Josiah's political demands. Andy Simpson pays the price of his naïvety, and it symbolizes the price that must be paid by the whole unhappy society of the island, from the inarticulate, frightened and resentful populace to the worried and lonely president himself. In this larger sense, then, the price is assessed in the end by Abrahams in terms of liberal values, and it is expressed as a breakdown in communication at all levels—between Josiah and the masses, between Andy Simpson and Josiah, Andy and Martha, Martha and Joel Sterning, Martha and Max Johnson. In other words, the contradiction Abrahams finds himself caught up in is a fairly inevitable one for the contemporary political novelist: in the novel he subjects the liberal ideology to various tests, finds it wanting, but ends by judging the entire situation in terms of it. It is a pessimistic vision, which seems to rest on a plausible interpretation of contemporary history, and an adequate idea of human nature. There is one important weakness in the intellectual structure, however, and it is characteristically dangerous because it represents the growth of a particular attitude in Abrahams' writing, the scope or potential meaning of which seems to elude his consciousness. Very soon after the death of the old president is announced, Joel Sterning and his wife Clara drive from their mountainside home to Clara's father's house for an emergency meeting of the board of Isaacs Enterprises. It is night, and on the way they encounter a great concourse of people making their way into the town on foot, towards the presidential palace.

> Then they reached the outskirts of the town and it was as no other night they had ever known. There were people everywhere. They moved like a flowing stream down from the hills that made up the hinterland and backbone and heart of the island: a silent stream of black peasant humanity.
>
> Clara looked at Joel for explanation.
>
> 'I think they're going to the Palace,' he said.
>
> 'They're so silent,' she said.
>
> 'Be careful. Don't blow your horn. Take the first side turning. It may be like this on the other main roads too, so we'd better make our way by the side roads.'
>
> 'They're not hostile,' she said.
>
> 'Just bewildered,' he said. 'Like a household of small children who have lost mother and father.'
>
> 'I know;' she said. 'They are frightened; and like all frightened creatures they are likely to panic and run amok at the slightest shock. We'll have to be careful.'[1]

The patronizing tone present in this extract reminds one immediately of the similar difficulties encountered with large groups of 'ordinary people' in Abrahams' earlier work, particularly, perhaps, of the romanticized nonsense about the 'masses' in *A Night of Their Own*. As we have repeatedly pointed out, *A Night of Their Own* is a special case, and Abrahams' unconvincingly stated positive attitude to those large segments of humanity, sometimes dignified by the title of 'the masses', nowhere conceals his essential isolation and remoteness from them—an isolation which has its roots in a rejection based on fear. If one were given to the sport of psychologizing, one

---

[1] *Ibid.*, p. 27.

might propound the theory that this fear is actually a fear of returning to the unpleasant conditions of his childhood; in this, of course, Abrahams would be far from unique.

In any event, this attitude develops to a forcefulness of expression that is sometimes startling and often distasteful in *This Island Now*. Distasteful not from any ideological point of view, (except perhaps from that of the broadest, most non-doctrinaire liberalism that wishes to avoid generalizations about large groups of people), but because it is never based on evidence that is accessible to the reader, even through the eyes of a reliable narrator. Needless to say, no attempt is made to examine or develop the character of any member of this group. Martha Lee has, of course, plenty to say about 'them', but her views on the subject are very reminiscent of the mystifications of *A Night of Their Own*, only much sharper and more negative. They probably approximate closely to Abrahams' own rather confused feelings. This is how she encounters the same crowds that hold up Joel and Clara in their car on the night of Moses Joshua's death:

> For them this night will never end, the woman told herself. They will weave a legend out of the happenings of this night, and with the legend they will bind and imprison their minds and make it easy for someone else to come and gain ascendency over them, as that dead old man in the Palace had done. She wanted to feel angry with them, but she could not. This is how they are, and to be angry with them is to be angry with man, and with God, and with life.[1]

A little later, as she circulates in the crowd, the following encounter takes place:

> A woman put a hand on Martha Lee's arm, leaned towards her ear and shouted: 'You see him? Them let you in?'
> 'No!' Martha shouted.
> 'Me wan'see him! We wan'see him! Him belong wid we!'
> 'You will!' Martha shouted. 'You will! In the morning!'

---

[1] *Ibid.*, p. 43.

'What?'

'In the morning! You will see him!'

'We wait! You see him?'

'No!'

'Don' go'way!' the woman patted her reassuringly. 'You will!'[1]

This is anecdotal, patronizing, offensive: the reader is given no chance to judge for himself. (It is also the nearest thing to a comic moment in the book.) And even though she reprimands Andy Simpson for appearing to 'dismiss' the hill peasants, her own attitude undergoes no development. At one stage with Joel she goes into a country bar and ingratiates herself with four middle-aged peasants; as soon as she tries to sound out their political opinions, not unnaturally, they become non-committal and reject her overtures. With the arrogance of a true bourgeois liberal, she ignores what her own response might have been in similar circumstances. Afterwards Joel says to her:

'You knew it would be like that; that they would not commit themselves, that they would bend with the wind.'

'I knew,' she said remotely.

'Then why let it cut you up as well?'

'As well?'

'You know what I mean: as well as everything else.'

'But it is everything for me, Joel. Do you still not understand that? Everything is part of what you call it.'

'This commitment to people who will not face reality? Who run away from everything? Who will only say what they know you want them to say? Who are always on the side of those in power. . .'

'Yes!' she said, angry now, with the kind of blazing anger he had seen in her before. 'They're all that and more! I can make a longer list of their faults than you can! But you are not qualified to name that list because you are not committed to them!. . . Oh, God! Oh God! I'm sorry, Joel. . .'

'But it's true,' he said sadly.

---

[1] *Ibid.*, p. 47.

After that they were silent till they left the hills and were back on the plain. Then Martha touched his hand briefly.

'Those men up there, Joel, they are the measure of our failure; they are uncommitted because throughout their history every decent impulse in them has been used as a tool to exploit them. And we, the decent people, have failed to give them faith in themselves and in their own dreaming. That is our failure, Joel.'[1]

The flash of insight and honesty in the last paragraph cannot really make up for her social gaucherie in her encounter with the farmers: what is worst of all, she has in a sense approached them instrumentally, not as men but as representatives of a group. Abrahams seems to be unaware of this, the basis of Martha's inability to communicate with her beloved 'little men'. Her lecture to her maid on the race problem, quoted earlier, is part of the same phenomenon.

What this boils down to, in fact, is a closer examination of the values of Abrahams' chief spokeswoman. The embattled third world liberal intellectual, whose commitment emerges as something involuntary, a product of birth and pigmentation, and is in any event a commitment to something less than action: who fails in her own terms the crucial test of communication with anyone outside a small group of people with similar backgrounds and interests, and whose profoundly pessimistic and negative judgments about other people are based on two things: the criterion of race and her own inability to make contact with the mass of the people to whom she regards herself as being committed. A glance at two passages should clinch the case against her, on the grounds of sloppy thinking, at least: it is Abrahams, perhaps, who must be accused of self-indulgence.

Martha Lee noted the cool detachment with which Max Johnson examined her and realized how wrong she had been to assume his involvement. For all his years, here, for all his great love of a woman of the island, this one had never made, will never make that commitment to the land which is a thing of the

---

[1] *Ibid.*, pp. 86–7.

heart and of the mind and of the soul—a wayward thing of dreaming and feeling that sought to establish a link with time and the earth and which would make more of a man's existence than just the brief moment of consciousness we call life.[1]

and:

She had wanted the parting to be on a warmer note for she knew that Max had just gone into a lonely exile for which nothing would compensate. She knew that at bedrock, when stripped of all the jingoistic rubbish of race and class and colour and nationality, all humans were plain people; made richer and more beautiful by their variety, but still only people; the same under the skin. And yet the history of the skin thing and what lay behind it had made for an invisible wall that had made impossible a parting on a warmer, more personal, more human note. He had, she knew now, always been the stranger within the gate for her and many others like her: and it was not a thing of her wanting or his wanting. It was so because of what had happened long before they were born. And so what you would give your heart and mind to, what you would do as an act of will, what you would do as a man using the blessed gift of conscious intelligence, is denied you because of a past over which you had no control, for which you have no responsibility.

Awareness of this was no new experience for Martha Lee; but it was personal now, and sharp and clearcut. It brought the anguish and the despair known only to the creature that knew it was trapped in a hopeless situation. Perhaps for others, coming later a point in time would be reached when there are no stranger within the gate anywhere on this earth of ours.[2]

In each of the passages, particularly the first, the tendency to purple is embarrassingly powerful, but the small kernel of substantive meaning is very elusive. Abrahams places his heroine in a situation more hopeless than it needs to be. The likely reason for this is that he himself fails the test of communication —his growing, almost obsessive distaste for 'the masses', lead-

---

[1] *Ibid.*, p. 185.   [2] *Ibid.*, p. 242.

ing to an inability to render his characters within a realistic imaginative context, makes it impossible for him to express with adequacy any version of the liberal vision. That is perhaps why only Maxwell Johnson, the conservative romantic, emerges with conviction as a living character.

9

Conclusion

Of all the writers in English in the field defined as 'African literature' none is as 'European' as Peter Abrahams, in regard to intellectual as well as artistic development. His participation in the drama of contemporary history began in the 'thirties, and quite early on he transferred his physical base to Europe; and the progress of his development as a writer has followed a European pattern characteristic of his generation. The initial commitment to Marxism as the most hopeful means of bringing about justice and social change gives way fairly early to a relatively uncritical adherence to the values of the Cold War, which is expressed in a manner entirely characteristic of a great many disillusioned fellow-travellers who became luminaries of the liberal world in the 'fifties, in writings such as his article 'The Blacks', which is part criticism, part apologia, for the treatment of Jomo Kenyatta during the Mau Mau period, and also presents a markedly unsympathetic picture of Kwame Nkrumah in the early days of his rule[1]; as well as in the long statement of his personal position on race and colour broadcast on the BBC and published in *Return to Goli* (analysed above, see pp. 99 ff).

By the end of that weary decade, however, the dedication to the West has worn thin; Abrahams himself has moved on, this time to Jamaica, and a long novelistic silence, possibly born out of the doubts and uncertainties that characterize the liberal

---

[1] 'The Blacks', article in *An African Treasury*, ed. Langston Hughes (Victor Gollancz, London, 1961). See also Abrahams: 'The Conflict of Culture in Africa', in *Phylon* (University of Atlanta, Vol. 16, no. 4, 1955), pp. 387–96 (reprinted from *International Affairs*, Vol. XXX, no. 3, July 1954).

position, as well as further disillusion, is broken by a highly emotional fictive outburst prompted by events in the one arena where certainty is not only a possibility but a moral imperative—South Africa. Almost immediately afterwards comes another novel, like its predecessor tied closely to a real-life situation with which the author has become intimate. This one, unlike *A Night of Their Own*, makes no attempt to hide the painful moral incertitude which characterizes the contemporary liberal situation, and ends in the sort of paralysis that is only too frequently the outcome. This paralysis is paralleled in the author's life by another long silence, which happened before, also during a period of disillusion: and we are left with the picture of a man of the utmost intellectual and moral sincerity and earnestness, lacking the imaginative power to liberate himself in his work from the interpretation of fairly close personal experience, against the background of the contemporary agony in personal and racial relations, perhaps doomed to the commission of what another honest man born into a grotesque situation, Isaac Babel, condemned in himself as 'the crime of silence'. There are abundant symptoms that it is becoming impossible for the orthodox novelist to interpret the monstrosities of current reality with 'the instruments at our disposal'; greater talent than Abrahams possesses fails to overcome identical difficulties (as perhaps Saul Bellow, who admires Abrahams' work, shows in the puzzling failure of *Mr Sammler's Planet*—a novel whose preoccupations are almost precisely those of Abrahams in *This Island Now* and *A Night Of Their Own*).

It may, paradoxically, fall to the inheritors of that tradition of which C. P. Snow saw Abrahams as forerunner[1] to do for the Western novel what the West can no longer do; and it is a familiar kind of irony that Abrahams, the pioneer, came too early to avoid being absorbed into the dominant stream, and was thus incapable of fulfilling the task in his own work.

---

[1] *Sunday Times* (London), 20 May 1951. In a famous review of *Wild Conquest*, Snow wrote that the book 'may be the forerunner of an entire school of African literary art'.

CRITICAL READING

(This list is not necessarily inclusive; mention of an article is certainly not synonymous with recommendation.)

Cartey, Wilfred: *Whispers from a Continent*. The literature of contemporary black Africa. (Heinemann Educational Books, 1971).

Heywood, Christopher: 'The novels of Peter Abrahams', in *Perspectives on African Literature* (selections from the proceedings of the Conference on African Literature held at the University of Ife, 1968), ed. C. Heywood (Heinemann/University of Ife Press, 1971).

Klima, Vladimir: *South African Prose Writing in English* (Prague, 1971).

Lewis, Primila: 'Politics and the Novel—an appreciation of *A Wreath for Udomo* and *This Island Now*', in *Zuka*, journal of East African creative writing (no. 2, May 1968, OUP, Nairobi).

Mphahlele, Ezekiel: *The African Image* (Faber and Faber, 1962).

Ravenscroft, Arthur: 'African Literature V: Novels of disillusion', in *Journal of Commonwealth Literature* (no. 6, January 1969).

Tucker, Martin: *Africa in Modern Literature* (N.Y., Ungar, 1967).

Wauthier, Claude: *The Literature and Thought of Modern Africa: a survey* (Pall Mall, 1966).

Appendix

The problem of rendering realistically characters of a completely different social or historical ambience from the author's or his audience's is certainly not confined to the world of the 'African' novel, though the historic situation of writers in this field brings them up against it less out of choice than necessity. The reasons for this are obvious: African novelists will write about African experience, by and large, and frequently, if not usually, with a non-African audience in mind. But the writers themselves tend sometimes to be much removed, in time or situation, from the characters or life they are describing: that this may be especially true of 'historical plots' is exemplified by both Chinua Achebe in *Things Fall Apart* and *Arrow of God*, and James Ngugi in *The River Between*. As usual, Abrahams is in this respect something of a special case: a non-white writing about South Africa may be obliged by the demands of his goal to render the conditions of African life (in the strict sense of the term) in that society, whether historic or contemporary, traditional or modern. But Abrahams has never experienced African life in South Africa from the inside, because of the powerful artificial barriers erected between the various groups of the population by the laws of apartheid. So in fulfilment of his early attempt to be definitive about the South African experience, he had to cast about for ways and means of rendering non-white characters successfully, especially after his failure in this area in all of his first three novels. In *Wild Conquest*, his most ambitious South African project, he was faced with the difficulty of both time and situation, and looked for verisimilitude to the work of another author, an African who, though an intellectual, was not so very far removed from his traditional background.

This was Solomon T. Plaatje, the journalist, political leader and linguist, who published in 1930 a novel called *Mhudi*, subtitled *An Epic of South African Native Life a Hundred Years Ago*. The novel is described in most of the standard critical surveys: it is not a literary success, technically or stylistically speaking, but Plaatje was not afraid of dialogue, and went into some detail regarding the customs and ceremonies and general behaviour of a people Abrahams was much interested in—the Matabele.

Abrahams drew heavily on Plaatje's novel for his Matabele characters and scenes. He introduces the Matabele to the reader, at the beginning of the section called 'Bayete!', with the episode of the murder of two of Mzilikazi's messengers, Bhoya and Bangela, by members of a subject tribe. This episode is taken straight from *Mhudi*, but it is interesting to see how Abrahams reworks his raw material. The first extract given below is from *Mhudi* and the second is Abrahams' presentation of it in *Wild Conquest*.

Mzilikazi's tribe originally was a branch of the Zulu nation which Chaka once ruled with an iron rod. Irritated by the stern rule of that monarch, Mzilikazi led out his own people who thereupon broke away from Chaka's rule and turned their faces westward.

Sweeping through the northern areas of Port Natal, they advanced along both banks of the Vaal River, driving terror into man and beast with whom they came in contact. They continued their march very much like a swarm of locusts; scattering the Swazies, terrifying the Basuto and the Bapedi on their outposts. They drove them back to the mountains at the point of the assegai; and, trekking through the heart of the Transvaal, they eventually invaded Bechuanaland where they reduced the natives to submission.

At length the Matebele established as their capital the city of Inzwinyani in Bahurutshe territory, the Bechuana inhabitants being permitted to remain on condition that their chiefs should pay tribute to Mzilikazi. Gradually enlarging their dominion, the Matebele enforced taxation first upon one and then another of the surrounding Bechuana clans, including the Barolong at Kunana, whose chief at the time was Tauana.

Perhaps the new administration might have worked well enough; but, unfortunately, the conquerors not only imported a fresh discipline but they also introduced manners that were extremely offensive even for these primitive people. For instance, the victorious soldiers were in the habit of walking about in their birthday garb thereby forcing the modest Bechuana women and children to retire on each appearance of Matebele men. This hide-and-seek life, which proved more inconvenient than accommodating, was ill calculated to inspire respect for the new authority. Needless to say, this outrage so shocking to local susceptibilities, was resented by the original population and became a perpetual source of discontent. Still, the new discipline was not stern; and as long as each chief paid taxes each spring time in acknowledgment of his fealty to Mzilikazi, the Bechuana were left in undisturbed possession of their old homes and haunts.

One of Tauana's right-hand men was a wealthy chieftain, Notto by name. Besides his home in the capital he owned three cattle stations and many cornfields in the country. His son, Ra-Thaga, minded one of the herds at a place called Mhuhucho.

One day, Notto set out to spend some time in the country with his son in order to fulfil his pastoral duties, such as ear-marking lambs and calves and braying skins and rheims. One morning, while Notto was engaged in these occupations at the cattle-post, two men came from Kunana who walked like bearers of very important news. After greeting him they related this startling information:

'Two Matebele *indunas*, Bhoya and Bangela, had come to Kunana to gather the annual tribute. They duly announced the object of their visit and asked that six young men should be supplied to carry the Barolong tribute for them and lay it "at the feet of Mzilikazi, ruler of earth and skies."

'Chief Tauana,' the messengers went on, 'received the visitors with indifference and, without informing his counsellors in any way, he commanded some young men to take the two to the ravine and "lose them," which is equivalent to a death sentence. The tax collectors were dragged away without notice and almost before they realized their doom they were stabbed to death.

'I am told,' said the narrator, 'that, before his death, Bhoya, with hands manacled, gesticulated and cried: "You dogs of a Western breed, you are going to suffer for this. You shall pay with your own blood and the blood of your children for laying your base hands on the courier of King Mzilikazi. A Matebele's blood never mingled with the earth without portending death and destruction. Kill me with your accursed hands, you menial descendants of mercenary hammersmiths, and you have sown the seed of your own doom. Do your hear me?"

'He was still speaking when Rauwe stabbed him in the breast. He fell forward, gave a gasp and a groan, rolled up the whites of his large dull eyes, and after uttering a dread imprecation, sank back lifeless.

'You can well understand,' said the emissary, 'that Mzilikazi is not going to take such treatment lying down; consequently the chief counsellors decided to take immediate steps to make amends. But as the chief would probably refuse to apologize, it was decided to summon home from the cattle posts all men of influence, to attend a tribal picho and arrange a settlement before it is too late.'[1]

The two men passed through, erect, looking straight in front of them. They carried themselves with the dignity of Matabele warriors. They were on the king's business. The king's dignity had to be upheld. They moved on till they were in the centre of Kunana. They knew that Barolong men and women and children followed at a safe distance, but they moved as though only they trod the earth.

At the centre of the city was a cluster of huts, larger and more decoratively built than the others. This was the seat of Tauana, chief of the Barolong.

Here they stopped and waited. A young man came out of the biggest hut, saw them, and went in again.

Tauana came out. He was short and fat and looked amiable. He was dead drunk. Two men brought a chair forward and he slumped into it. He raised drunken eyes to the two men.

'Greetings, Tauana!' Bhoya said.

The chief of the Barolong remained silent. Bhoya's eyes flashed.

'I bring the greetings of Mzilikazi!' Bhoya said sharply. 'Mzilikazi the great, lord of the leopard and the lion, master of the elephant, king of the mountains and the valleys, eater of the jackal, destroyer of his enemies, protector of his friends!'

Taunana hiccoughed. He turned to one of his young men.

---

[1] S. T. Plaatje *Mhubi* (Lovedale Press, South Africa, 1930), pp. 4–7.

'Rauwe, I see the naked men are covered today. They must realize at last that our women don't like to see their nakedness, hah? Or is it cold, hah?'

Rauwe laughed. The people waited in silence.

Bhoya said: 'You are drunk, old man! It pleases you to insult Mzilikazi but tomorrow you will weep. It is the king's wish that you and your people deliver to him, as tribute, a hundred head of milking cows and a hundred head of fat sheep. You are, further, to supply men to drive these to the king's city!'

Tauana tossed his head in drunken anger.

'Taxes! Taxes all the time! I am sick of your taxes. Before you people with your nakedness came from the East we lived without paying any taxes to anyone and we were happy, heh, Rauwe?'

'But you were attacked and robbed of your cattle and your people were killed. Now you are protected by the shadow of Mzilikazi!'

'That is no matter,' Tauana said. 'We were free, we were happy. We didn't give our cattle to anyone. We kept them for ourselves. I am sick of you and your king and your taxes! I want you to be lost. Understand? I want you to be lost.'

Bhoya turned his eyes to the young men who had drawn near.

'Think you! Your chief is drunk. To disobey Mzilikazi is to invite a death that is swift and sudden. There will not be a child left or a wall that is not crushed after the Matabele warriors have passed through here! Tell your chief to obey the orders of Mzilikazi or those of you who are fortunate enough to escape will mourn this day for all eternity.'

Tauana turned to his young men.

'The ravine is close by, Rauwe. Lose these collectors of taxes! I hate taxes!'

The young men moved forward. Bhoya and Bangela were unarmed.

Bhoya said: 'I have warned you. You share in the madness of your chief. I am sorry for you, you descendants of hammer-smiths! Kill us and you sow the seed of your own destruction. A Matabele's blood never mingles with the earth without calling forth death and destruction. I have warned you!'

Rauwe struck Bhoya across the face with the handle of a knife. Others tied their hands and dragged them to the ravine on the western edge of the city. There, Rauwe stabbed Bhoya in the chest while a companion stabbed Bangela.

Bhoya shouted: '*Bayete!*'

Then they pushed him over.

Bangela echoed the cry in a dying breath.

The young men, led by Rauwe, returned, singing songs of battle. Tauana got up to receive them.

'Death to all tax collectors!' he shouted drunkenly. 'Beer for my soldiers! We will show these naked easterners!'

He led the young men into his hut.

'Beer! Beer!' He kept up the call till beer was brought.

'Drink, my soldiers, drink!'

They drank deeply and sang. Such a long time they had been under the heel of the Matabele. Such a wonderful feeling to turn on the oppressor.

But outside there were those who were sober, those who could think calmly of the power of the Matabele. Among them, the word went round:

Tauana had ordered the death of Mzilikazi's messengers. The young men had obeyed.

And each time it was told, the menace inherent in the deed grew.

Two of Mzilikazi's messengers were dead.

It hung over Kunana and the hut of Tauana was a drunken island in a sea of fear. It spread till it reached the elders at the cattle posts on the outskirts of the city.

When night fell Kunana was a throbbing hive of fear. People acted, talked, and ate their food as though they were walking a tight-rope. And in every mind, except those in the hut of Tauana, were the questions: What would happen? When? What could they do to avoid it?

The elders held a meeting.

'What are we to do?' one asked.

The most respected among them, an owner of much cattle and land, a wise man called Notto, said:

'There is only one thing to do. We must go to Mzilikazi. We must take him double the tribute he demanded. We must

P

get Tauana to lead us. We must make him throw himself on Mzilikazi's mercy. There is no other way.'[1]

What Abrahams has done, obviously, is to dramatize Plaatje's bald narration, which is much more the raw material of fiction than fiction itself. Abrahams works most of the information about the Matabele into the dialogue. He creates an atmosphere through the use of detail, as in the manner of walking adopted by Mzilikazi's emissaries when they enter the subject town: and emphasizes the folly and impotence of Tauana by making him a drunken sot.

The most fundamental change, of course, is that Abrahams does not mediate the episode through the device of reported speech but presents it directly, thus providing a dramatic framework for his characters and dialogue.

It is a little difficult to accept that the two passages demand the same kind of literary judgment: Abrahams is so obviously the professional while Plaatje doesn't get much beyond the novelist *manqué*. By these standards, however, it might be argued that Abrahams is the one who appears least successful, because while as far as structure is concerned he has provided Plaatje's dry report with an acceptable fictive framework, in terms of dialogue and characterization he is at best stilted and at worst slapdash. A paragraph such as this one: 'They drank deeply and sang. Such a long time they had been under the heel of the Matabele. Such a wonderful feeling to turn on the oppressor' constitutes a virtual denial of dramatic possibilities in its alarming perfunctoriness. It is a complete failure of the intensity needed for successful novelistic shorthand. Abrahams does not seem to care: the difficulty at this stage appears already in something like its later form in his subsequent work—an inability to become involved in the fate of characters very different in situation and preoccupation from himself. The most immediate and

---

[1] *Wild Conquest*, pp. 153–4.

telling form of the difficulty is in dialogue: but the failure is a much deeper one than that, and constitutes a serious flaw in the novelistic imagination itself, rather than a mere technical shortcoming.

The other major borrowing from *Mhudi* is found in the description of the feast at Inzwinyani, Mzilikazi's capital, after the destruction of Kunana, which is described on pp. 34–7 in *Mhudi* and 190–201 in *Wild Conquest.* Abrahams takes his praise-song (p. 190) straight from Plaatje, and most of the events of the feast, in particular the speeches of praise at Langa's triumph and the dissentient note sounded by Gubuza, the king's general, come from the same source. The disagreement between Gubuza and the other generals is papered over in the same way in both books, through a diplomatic speech by Mzilikazi, in which Abrahams follows Plaatje closely, clarifying his syntax and simplifying the presentation somewhat. Where there is a significant change it is in the two sets of reasons given by Gubuza for throwing cold water on Langa's triumph. In Plaatje's version, he is revealed as a legalist who operates entirely within the traditional framework.

> He said, 'No my chiefs, I am not so hopeful as the previous speakers. Gubuza has sat at the feet of many a wise man; I have been to Zululand, to Swaziland, to Tongaland and to Basutoland. I know the northern forests, I know the western deserts and I know the eastern and southern seas. Wiseacres of different nationalities are agreed that cheap successes are always followed by grievous aftermaths. Old people likewise declare that individuals, especially nations, should beware of the impetuosity of youth. Are we sure that Bhoya was guiltless?' he asked. 'Was there provocation? Supposing there was, are we satisfied that the Barolong could have maintained order in any manner short of killing Bhoya and his companion? Did Bhoya simply deliver his message or did he violate Barolong rights in any way? Did he not perhaps terrorize the children or molest Barolong women? My Lords and my Chiefs, I am a King's servant and know what I am talking about. I ask these questions because men of my circle too often forget that they are

emissaries of the King. They sometimes think that they are their own ambassadors; they are too apt to forget that without their ambassadorship they are but menials of low station. Royal appointments have on some of them the same effect as strong drink in the head of other men.'

By this time the buzz of dissenting voices was making it positively difficult to follow the speaker, who continued amid frequent interruptions. 'I have heard nothing from previous speakers to indicate that the Prince had asked Tauana for any reasons; nothing to show that he would not in due course have appeared in Inzwinyani and explained his action.'[1]

Abrahams exploits the possibilities more thoroughly, in accordance with his more sophisticated frame of reference. His Gubuza emerges as a humanist who values life more than the form of pomp owing to a king.

'I have listened to the words of Sitonga, my brothers, and I do not like them.' He waited till they were silent again. 'I am the king's man. You all know that. Murmur if you will, but know I am the king's man. As the king's man, I will speak what is in my heart. I will not use the powerful art of oratory to sway you, my children. My speech will be brief. After me others can sway you. I will not tell you of all the things I have shared with Mzilikazi. I will not tell you of the battles we fought together or the joys we have shared. This is not a time for that.

'I said I do not like the words of Sitonga. I say it again. I, Gubuza, have sat at the feet of many wise men. I have listened to their words, and I have learned wisdom from them.

'I was born in Zululand. Lately, I have been there again, not as Gubuza, Commander of the king's armies, but as an ordinary man with no name. I have been to Swaziland, to Tongaland and to Basutoland. I know the northern forests, I know the western deserts, I know the eastern and the southern seas. I have made these journeys, not on a whim, but in search of wisdom. It is with this wisdom that I say I do not like the words of Sitonga.

'Children of the Matabele!' A more personally angry

---

[1] *Mhudi*, pp. 40–1.

note crept into his voice. 'Wise men of different tribes and nationalities are agreed that cheap successes are nearly always followed by the shadow of tragedy. Wise men are agreed that nations should in their strength tread carefully. My friend, Moshesh, king of the Basutos, can tell much of this wisdom. He is, this day, building a nation dedicated to the wisdom of treading carefully in strength.'

Again there was uproar. It started somewhere near Tabata. Gubuza calmly waited till it passed.

'I hear scorn at the name of Moshesh. Listen, children! When the name of Gubuza, and many another, is long forgotten, men will tell of the wisdom of Moshesh. Scorn not that name for in doing so you show your own stupidity. For myself, I wish that I had stayed longer with that wise man.

'I hurried back when word reached me of this affair at Kunana for my heart was sore within me. I asked myself, and I ask you now. Are we sure that Bhoya and his companion were guiltless? Was there no provocation? If they were guiltless, was there no other answer? Word reached me that Tauana was drunk, that he had not taken counsel from his elders. What had those elders decided? Who among you has not done wrong in a drunken moment? I have.

'Do we know if the people of Kunana had decided to punish their own chief and make amends for the death of our two *indunas*? My lord and my people—'[1]

Again the rhetoric is intensified. The question is whether Abrahams justifies his forcing of the Matabele warrior into the mould of the modern humanist political sage.

Plaatje's Gubuza's tactical retreat when opinion is going against him simply confirms his traditionalism. His chief virtue is that of caution, the sincere conservative's trustiest weapon.

Gubuza made a reluctant reply. He said, 'I am sorry if my words wounded the feelings of the chiefs. When I spoke this morning, I had seen some of the cattle but was not then aware that the booty was so large. When I reached the plateau and

---

[1] *Wild Conquest*, pp. 195–6.

saw the swarms of Barolong cattle I felt a quiver on my breast as though it had been touched by a spear; for I am convinced that the owners of so many cattle will never rest until they recover them. It should not be forgotten that all these cattle belonged to men and not to children. It is clear that they increased and multiplied under the wands of clever magicians or they would never have bred in such abundance. We know not the manner in which the Barolong prepared their spells, and I shudder when I think of the day when the revengeful owners of those herds will come back for them. The carousals of those who are now enjoying themselves outside will not save us from their wrath.'[1]

Abrahams again does the opposite, making his Gubuza into a rationalist prophet set against the background of witchcraft and ignorance:

'I hear the word coward! I have my shield! I have my spear! Let any man here step forward and touch spears with me!'

In the hush that followed, everybody waited, but no man came. Gubuza's lips curled. He turned to the throne.

'No doubt we are all drunk with the size of the booty and the good beer of our women,' he paused and weighed his next words: 'But, my lord, I am afraid we have only made a fresh enemy and one day we will pay for it.'[2]

There are two obvious questions. Is this plagiarism? And can Abrahams force Gubuza and Mkomozi into the mould he wants without violating the canons of literary realism? Although the second is by far the most interesting of the two, it is not unrelated to the issues raised by the first.

One may argue that a historical novelist can do virtually whatever he likes with his characters in terms of moral or philosophical issues as long as he maintains the necessary degree of literary verisimilitude. This is rather an extreme

[1] *Mhudi*, p. 45.
[2] *Wild Conquest*, p. 198.

point of view, but I adopt it with a purpose. One may accept Abrahams' methodology in producing the degree of verisimilitude, e.g. Mkomozi or Gubuza must speak in rather stilted, Old Testament prophetic tones because they have a prophetic function. But can one also swallow the next step and insist that this is independent of what they prophesy? Plaatje's range of expression was much more limited than Abrahams', but the stilted formality of his speakers (in itself less successful as dialogue than Abrahams' efforts) at least has an organic relationship to the *meaning* of what they say. To go one step further, it is possible to suspect that the content of their speeches is altogether more probable than that of Abrahams' Gubuza or Mkomozi. In other words, it is unlikely that anyone at Mzilikazi's court was a liberal humanist with empiricist leanings. Making a character speak like a minor prophet does not increase his inherent plausibility.

Thus plagiarism, which I would take to mean on an instance like this the blatant theft of another man's work, ideas and methods for no independent artistic purpose, does not arise. (My judgment in an article published in 1968 was unwarrantedly severe.) But Abrahams is guilty of a different kind of failure: while his purpose *is* independent of Plaatje's, subordinate to a larger whole, he fails to achieve it in general terms, and specifically fails to render credible the use to which he puts Plaatje's material. The transformation does not succeed, and one of the more ironic effects is to give these passages the ring of insincerity, though of course it would be unfair to judge the work or its author in these terms, since the total conception of this novel is wholly sincere.

Bibliography

Dark Testament (short stories)
George Allen & Unwin Ltd, London, 1942

Song of the City (novel)
Dorothy Crisp & Co., London, 1945

Mine Boy (novel)
Dorothy Crisp & Co., London, 1946
Faber and Faber, London, 1954
Heinemann Educational Books, London, 1963

The Path of Thunder (novel)
Harper, New York, 1948
Faber and Faber, London, 1952

Wild Conquest (novel)
Harper, New York, 1950
Faber and Faber, London, 1951

Return to Goli (documentary)
Faber and Faber, London, 1953

Tell Freedom (autobiography)
Faber and Faber, London, 1954
Collier-Macmillan, New York, 1970

A Wreath for Udomo (novel)
Faber and Faber, London, 1956

Jamaica: Island Mosaic (documentary)
Her Majesty's Stationery Office (Corona Library Series),
London, 1957

A Night of Their Own (novel)
Faber and Faber, London, 1965

This Island Now (novel)
Faber and Faber, London, 1966

American dates of publication are given only when they influence the order of appearance of Abrahams' works.

Index

compiled by Vera Varley